SUSANVILLE

The Roops, The Arnolds
&
A Girl Named Susan

SANDRA JONAS

Cover Design: Antelope Design
Cover Photo: Winter scene
looking south from Susanville
toward the Diamond Mountains
in the very northern part of the Sierras.
From a postcard donated by Susan's granddaughter,
Zellamae Arnold Miles

PronghornPress.org

Susan Roop
Courtesy of Lassen County Historical Society

Table of Contents

Illustrations

SUSANVILLE

Introduction

I am the granddaughter of Susan Roop Arnold for whom Susanville is named. I never knew my grandmother, but as a young girl I enjoyed the stories my father, Medford "Med" Roop Arnold shared about his mother. Med was the youngest of eight children, born when Susan was forty-three years old. As Daddy was the baby of family, he was indulged by his parents, especially his mother. He often told me what a wonderful, caring mother Susan was.

Daddy told me that on numerous occasions when he awoke in the morning, he would find his mother on the back porch, cleaning up. She had just returned from spending the night caring for a sick friend. She always made sure she was home in time to make her children breakfast before school.

The importance of a good education was instilled in the Arnold children. In fact, as Med grew up he excelled in school and in sports. He was president of his senior class at Lassen High School, and later he attended Stanford where he received a teaching credential, and the University of Southern California

(USC) for his law degree. When he returned home to Susanville, Med married Zella May Spalding, a descendant of another prominent family active in the settlement of Susanville. My father was community minded and was a respected coach and teacher at both Lassen High School and Lassen College.

On behalf of the Roop-Arnold family, I want to thank Sandra Jonas for writing this book about Susan Roop Arnold. Little has been written about women in the settling of Susanville. Although much has been written and researched on Isaac Roop, Susanville's founder, little was known about his children until now. I am proud that my grandmother is honored with a book of her own. Collecting the information contained in these pages was something my family has wanted to do for many, many years, but for whatever reasons, it was never done. For her thorough research of Susan Roop Arnold's life, my family will always be indebted to Ms. Jonas.

Zellamae Arnold Miles

SUSANVILLE

Prologue

The town of Susanville is named in honor of Susan Roop Arnold. Susan was the only daughter of Isaac Roop who established the first trading post and settlement in the Honey Lake Valley. Referred to as "Rooptown", the small community was situated on the Nobles Emigrant Trail. By 1857 the Nobles was the preferred wagon route for emigrants who traveled west to the fertile valleys of Northern California.

Rooptown began to grow as settlers moved in and establish homesteads. In 1858 Isaac Roop renamed the town Susanville in honor of his much-loved daughter. Although Susan Roop did not arrive in Susanville until 1863, she spent the rest of her life there, dedicated to family and friends in the town whose residents respected and admired her.

This biography recounts the life of Susan Roop, as well as her extended family members, many of whom journeyed west during the Gold Rush and the Civil War years. America's brave pioneers of the nineteenth century, including Susan and her relatives, risked everything in search of new land and opportunity. Some found success and happiness while others lost their lives.

The Roops, The Arnolds & A Girl Named Susan

SUSANVILLE

Part I

The Roops, The Arnolds & A Girl Named Susan

SUSANVILLE

1

The Early Years

Ashland County, Ohio

1830s and Earlier

Many of the early settlers in Ashland County, Ohio, were of Pennsylvania German stock, as were both sets of Susan's grandparents, the Gardners and the Roops. Both families moved from the Eastern states into the Ohio Valley in the 1830s, seeking open and affordable land. Susan's grandparents all settled in Ashland County, located in the central plains region of Ohio. The expanse of rural land they settled on was made up of fields of level prairie and gently rolling hills, with an ideal climate for growing crops.

Lake Erie is located less than one hundred miles to the north of Ashland County. The Ohio River, which marks the state's southern boundary with Kentucky and West Virginia, is two hundred miles to the south. The Mohican River flows through

Ashland County and the early pioneers settled near the natural streams and lakes that teemed with fish. To the east along the Pennsylvania border are the Allegheny Mountains, a rugged expanse, forested in a variety of timber, primarily hardwoods. Early settlers found an abundance of wild game: deer, fowl, and fur-bearing animals, which added nourishment to the stew pot.

When the Gardner and Roop families arrived in north central Ohio in the late 1830s, their dwellings and barns were constructed of logs covered in clapboards. As more pioneers arrived and sawmills were built, family homes were framed of lumber and hewn logs. The fire hearths inside the dwellings were constructed for warmth and cooking, accomplished by either using a Dutch oven or a metal frame to hang the soup kettle over the fire.

The temperate climate in Ohio was pleasing to the newcomers who especially enjoyed the mild summers. When Susan's ancestors settled in Ashland County, it was originally a part of Richland County. Her mother's people—the Gardners—put down roots in Ohio in 1837, and her father's family—the Roops—in 1838.

Both families settled in the same vicinity on good level farmland in Montgomery Township. The community was originally called Uniontown when it was established in 1815. As with many immigrant groups, the German settlers in Ohio held on to their language and many customs brought from the old country.

SUSANVILLE

The Gardners

The Gardner ancestors settled in America in the mid-eighteenth century. It was a time of great influx of German immigrants. John, Susan's maternal grandfather, a wainwright (a wagon maker) by trade, was born circa 1799 in Pennsylvania.

Susan's mother, Nancy was born on December 20, 1822 to John and Jane (Cole) Gardner in Allegheny County, Pennsylvania. Nancy was the oldest of John and Jane's six children, and the only girl. Her siblings were John, James, George, Thomas, and David.

In the Pennsylvania Septennial Census of 1779-1863 the family is listed in Plum Township, Allegheny County in western Pennsylvania in the year 1800.

The Gardners were involved in small-scale farming and the raising of livestock, as were the majority of the residents. Allegheny County at that time was a hilly, wooded region where the tilled acreage tended to be small when cleared. John built and repaired wagons, and his older sons assisted him when they were not tending the livestock or working in the field.

All of the family members worked to ensure the success of the farmstead. The growing season was short in the Allegheny region. The meager soil quality and cool temperatures limited farm size and crop production. Families were barely able to make a living due to the financial depression in their state in the early 1800s. Pennsylvanians were pulling up roots and moving west. The Gardners were among the many families that joined the movement. After their third son was born in 1837, the Gardners moved to the Ohio Valley.

They settled in Montgomery Township, Richland County, and were listed in the 1840 U.S. Census. The climate in the area was preferable, and the moderate temperatures suited farming operations. They found the land to be open and level with quality soil for planting.

The family settled near Pleasant Ridge located five miles east of Ashland, in a small area referred to as Swineford's Corners. Farmers harvested many bushels of corn each year in the area where the Gardners settled. According his friends, John and Jane's oldest son, John Jr., also known as Johnnie Gardner, was an outgoing fellow.

The Roops

Susan's father, Isaac Roop was a descendant of German American immigrants who first settled in New York in the seventeenth century. After several generations, they moved to Lancaster, Pennsylvania. Isaac's grandfather, Joseph Roop, Sr., moved the family to Frederick County, Maryland after the Revolutionary War. The family was listed in the 1820 and the 1830 U.S. Federal Census in Frederick County, Maryland. In 1837, Carroll County was formed from the eastern section of Frederick County where the Roops lived.

Crowding in the Eastern states forced many families to seek affordable land to the west. Fertile acreage and open country enticed Isaac's father to sell their farm in Maryland and move to Ohio.

Joseph Roop, Jr. (hereafter referred to only as Joseph Roop) and Susannah Engle were married on January 8, 1816 in Frederick County, Maryland. Isaac (Susan's father) was the fourth of eleven children— nine sons and two daughters—born to Joseph and Susannah Roop. They were: Josiah, David, Ephraim, Isaac, Israel, John, Eli, Jonas, Elizabeth, Mary, and Joseph N.

In the summer of 1838 the Roops departed Carroll County, Maryland. Eager for adventure, Isaac, then sixteen, was excited to join the westward movement to the Ohio Valley region.

Families who left Maryland followed the National Road (also known as the Cumberland Road). They crossed the Allegheny Mountains, traveled through southwestern Pennsylvania to the Ohio River at West Virginia, and then crossed into Ohio. The journey from Maryland to Ohio took the Roops several weeks, and the well-leveled road made wagon travel tolerable. There were inns, mercantile stores, and taverns along the road where travelers could find food and accommodation. Entrepreneurs made a good living by selling essential supplies to the travelers.

Isaac made a mental note of the business transactions he observed. He learned a valuable life lesson on the trip: the merchants and businessmen earned a tidy profit from travelers headed west.

Joseph Roop, along with his wife and children, were among the early settlers in the eastern part of Montgomery Township, Richland County, Ohio. Having purchased the Pratt farm, the family became justly prosperous through their hard work of farming and raising livestock.

Joseph traveled yearly to sell his cattle in Medina County, a distance of approximately forty miles. He drove the wagon, and the livestock were herded along the route. To accompany him on the trip, he hired a young man who was paid to care for the cattle along the way. It was a long trek for the young stock, and Joseph's assistant often found it necessary to lift tired calves into the wagon during the two-week journey.

The Roops were pioneer members of the Church of the Brethren, also referred to as the Dunkards, whose members embraced the simple life. Isaac's father, Joseph, was an affluent and devout family man who donated the land on which the Dickey Church and Cemetery were located three miles southeast of Ashland.

In the 1840 U.S. Census the Roop family was listed in Montgomery, Richland County, Ohio, with eleven family members in the household. The two oldest sons had already established farms of their own.

David Roop and his wife Elizabeth also lived in Richland County on their own farm. They were near neighbors to Joseph Roop and John Gardner.

The oldest son, Josiah Roop, lived in Bloom Township, Seneca County, Ohio, in 1840. The Roop children worked hard on their new farm and were burdened with chores most days of the year. The children attended school during the winter months, after all the crops had been harvested and the fields were prepared for spring.

SUSANVILLE

Born in Ohio

The 1840s

When Isaac Roop married Nancy Gardner on December 24, 1840, both were a youthful eighteen years old. The holiday season of 1840 was a special one for Nancy as she celebrated both her birthday and her marriage in the same week.

Their first child, Susan Engle Roop was born on Saturday, November 13, 1841 in Montgomery Township, Ashland County, Ohio, to the delight of her parents. The young couple welcomed their first child eleven months after their marriage the previous Christmas Eve.

The Roops settled down to begin their future together. Isaac and Nancy settled close to family and friends, as early pioneers often did, associating themselves with others of like ancestry and religion. The young couple lived on a farm near his parents, and carried on the tradition of hardworking frontier farmers. With baby Susan they embraced home and family life.

When Isaac was not working at the family sawmill and gristmill, he could be found with his nose in a book and a pen in his hand. Roop family descendants have insisted that Isaac was educated, although scarcely, due to the time he spent farming as a boy. After his marriage, his young wife, who in her youth had been well educated, schooled him. With Nancy's tutoring, Isaac increased his proficiency in reading, writing, and public speaking—an aptitude that would prove useful to him in his later years.

Shortly after Susan turned two, Nancy gave birth to John Valentine Roop on November 27, 1843. Two years later on November 30, 1845, Isaiah Brian Roop was born. The household was blessed with three small children, who kept Nancy busy from dawn until dusk. The chores were constant and tiring, with food to cook, the garden to tend, animals to be fed, and clothing to make.

Isaac spent his days working at the mills, which were driven by waterwheels. The mills provided the basic products needed by the early settlers—lumber for cabins and barns, and processed grain that was ground for home cooking and animal feed.

Isaac's brothers, Josiah and Jonas Roop, had both settled in Seneca County, Ohio, by 1847. Jonas studied at Seneca County Academy in 1848 in Republic Ohio, located about fifty miles northwest of Ashland. Early in the spring of 1849, he taught his first school classes in Adams Township six miles north of Republic.

At the same time Jonas was teaching school, he studied medicine under the supervision of a local doctor. He then moved to Lucas County in northwest Ohio. He became acquainted with a young lady named Margaret Allen who, a few years later, would become his wife.

The Gold Rush
1849

Josiah Roop left his wife and children in Ohio and headed off to seek his fortune in California during the Gold Rush of 1849. A dozen men from Republic, including Josiah, departed from Cincinnati on April 13. The men traveled on board the *Belle of the West*, a fine sidewheel steamboat, which arrived in St. Louis on April 17. Josiah and the Republic Company met up with men from Xenia and Springfield, Ohio, who had also arrived at the Missouri River landing.

Approximately five thousand emigrants, including Josiah, along with his group of forty men, were all in position at Independence. They would start for the plains on May 10, 1849.

After stocking up on supplies, they began their journey on the overland trail west. When the men left the Great Plains and passed Fort Hall they then traveled along the California Trail. Josiah and the Ohio men passed along the Humboldt River and then over the Sierra Nevada. They arrived at the Yuba River in September of 1849.

During the fall of 1849, the men of the Republic Company spent day and night building a dam at Rose Bar. After a rocker and sluice box were assembled, they prepared to mine the riverbed below the dam. In October of 1849, Josiah and the Ohioans began to work their claim on the Yuba River. Unforeseen heavy rains demolished the dam and the mining equipment. Josiah lost most of his investment.

As soon as spring snows melted, the men set out for the Trinity Mountains where they panned for gold at Clear Creek. After one of the Ohio men died and another departed flat broke, Josiah headed out alone. He had time to mull over his options as he traveled to Bear River to check on the cows he'd left grazing there. Josiah, disheartened, concluded that prospecting for gold was backbreaking work and the payout elusive.

He decided to sell what he could and go into the mercantile business. He doubled his investment at the sale of his mining gear, and bought six yoke of oxen. He then traded for miner's tools and provisions, after he sold his own equipment that had not been destroyed at Rose Bar when the dam broke.

In the summer of 1850, Josiah established a general store at Shasta (formerly Reading Springs), situated at the north end of the Sacramento Valley, at the entrance to the northern mines. Josiah discovered that selling needed supplies to miners was a lucrative business.

SUSANVILLE

2

Until We Meet Again

Farewell

1850

Susan's mother, Nancy, only twenty-seven years old, died of typhoid fever on May 23, 1850. Nancy was buried in Eckley Cemetery, Vermillion Township, near Haynesville, Ohio, the oldest cemetery in Ashland City.

A widower, at the age of twenty-eight, Isaac was left with three young children to care for. Susan was eight years old, John was six, and little Isaiah was four. Grief and the impulsiveness of youth compelled Isaac to make a hasty life-changing decision.

By 1850 the gristmill was a failure, and Isaac had lost the income from the business, needed to support his family.

Joseph Roop had purchased the wood framed mill from John Hendricks. The mill was located below the mouth of Clear Creek on the Vermillion River. It was a simple water powered mill that had turned into a thriving business and good income for the family until 1850. Joseph and his sons dug a deep ditch from Lower Lake to increase the water flow to the mill. The only thing they succeeded in doing was draining the lake. Without water power, the mill was forced to close.

Isaac knew that if he stayed in Ohio, long days of farm work and meager pay lay ahead of him. His evenings would be consumed with chores and caring for the children. Isaac pondered his options silently. He was convinced that if he went to California, he could easily and quickly make enough money to support his family.

His decision was not made lightly, but thoughtfully. The health and wellbeing of his children was the most important consideration. Life in Ohio appeared bleak at best, making it easier for Isaac to leave than to stay.

He decided he would join his brother in California. Josiah was by then a successful merchant in Shasta. Josiah promised to help Isaac make a fresh start in the booming gold rush town. Until he was settled out West, Isaac would leave the children with close friends and family members.

By the time the census takers arrived in Ashland County in August of 1850, Isaac had sold what he could, and had packed up the house and children. In preparation for his departure, he moved into the home of his father-in-law (John Gardner), taking Susan with him. Since there was not sufficient space to keep the three children together in either the Gardner's home or Isaac's parents' farmhouse, the boys were fostered out with close friends, near to where their grandparents lived: John was placed with the Sheridan's, and Isaiah with the White family.

The 1850 U.S. Federal Census Montgomery Township, Ashland County, Ohio, enumerated August 12, 1850:

- John V. Gardner, wagon maker, age 51; real estate value $600; Jane Gardner, wife, age 50; John Gardner, age 20; James Gardner, age 17; George Gardner, age 13; Thomas Gardner, age 10; David Gardner, age 8; Isaac Roop, age 28; Susan Roop, age 8.
- John Roop, age 8; Paul Sheradden*, age 27; Martha Sheradden, wife age 25; George Sheradden, age 1.
- Isaiah Roop, age 4; Joshua White, blacksmith age 23; Catharine White, wife age 21.
- Joseph Roop, age 58; Susannah Roop, wife age 56; Ephraim Roop, age 29; Mary Roop, age 17; Elizabeth Roop, age 16; Joseph [N] Roop, age 14; Permelia Hopkins, age 54; Mary C. Noble, age 38.

The 1850 U.S. Federal Census Non Population Agriculture Schedule enumerated these details on August 9, 1850, Joseph Roop farm:

---

* There were various spellings of names in old records, as happened with the Sheridan surname

200 acres improved land
148 acres unimproved land
Cash value of farm, $12,000
Value of the farming implements
    and machinery, $200
Horses 20
Milk Cows 5
Other Cattle 4
Sheep 600
Swine 11
Value of Livestock, $1,200
Wheat bushels 500
Indian Corn bushels 500
Oats bushels 200
Pounds of Wool 2800
Irish Potatoes bushels 50
Butter pounds 200
Hay tons 100
Clover seed bushels 15
Value of the animals slaughtered, $120
Molasses gallons 15

Isaac Travels to California

During the first week of September 1850, Isaac bid his family farewell and departed Ohio for California. He chose to travel through the Isthmus of Panama, which, along with Nicaragua, were the two quickest routes to California at the time. When Isaac left Ohio in September, it was too late in the year to join a wagon train west, as all had departed in the

SUSANVILLE

spring. (The emigrants who departed on the overland crossing in May usually arrived in California in the month of September.)

Weekly newspaper accounts overflowed with reports of gold seekers who had journeyed west. Whether by land or sea, news excerpts enticed hopeful emigrants to join the rush for gold. On April 18, 1850, the *Wayne County Democrat* (Ohio) reported that in the previous twelve months almost eighty thousand men had departed for California. It also noted that between 1849 and 1850, five hundred ships had sailed the dangerous route around Cape Horn.

In the May 29, 1850 edition of the *Richland Shield and Banner* (Ohio) it was reported that fifteen thousand emigrants were positioned at the supply point of Council Bluffs, with three thousand teams in need of provisions for the journey.

Travel to California was difficult and dangerous. During the Gold Rush years, it was estimated that of those who set out, ten percent of the emigrants perished on the overland journey. Illness and accidents took the largest toll. The pioneers, who'd left the comfort of their homes, were willing to take the risk.

Travelers who chose the Central American route would spend less time in transit. It took approximately one to two months to cross the Isthmus through Panama or Nicaragua. The Isthmus crossing in Nicaragua totaled two hundred seventy eight miles, compared to forty-seven and a half miles across the Isthmus of Panama. Ships were commissioned to run the Atlantic and Pacific oceans, dropping passengers on either side of the Isthmus.

The overland crossing by wagon train averaged four to six months, and those who sailed around Cape Horn spent six to twelve months in passage. Isaac booked his passage in New York for travel to San Francisco through Panama. He was bound for Panama on Monday, September 9, 1850. The sidewheel steamer he boarded followed the North Atlantic current south. After passing into the Caribbean Sea, the ship soon anchored at the entrance of the Chagres River, at Colon, along the coast of Panama.

The passengers were left to fend for themselves on the dangerous Isthmus crossing. Their choices were to go by mule, canoe, or on foot. Travelers were often stranded in the heat of the Central American jungle as they searched for natives to assist them in the crossing. Those who arrived on time to rendezvous with their ships usually hired a mule and a canoe for the trip on steep, dense paths, and over waterways in Panama.

The jungles and swamps were filled with snakes and insects that spread yellow fever and malaria. At times the rainfall could be torrential, which made the muddy roads dreadful. The pathways were clogged with mules, people, packets of mail, and satchels of personal belongings. While some travelers trudged along the river path carrying their own luggage, others were fortunate enough to hire a native to transport them in a canoe, a simple hollowed out log that was used to haul bananas. Accidents and disease took their toll on the travelers.

SUSANVILLE

Isaac hired mule and river transports and arrived in Panama City in good time. He boarded a small launch that took him out to the steam ship, *Oregon* that lay anchored in the bay.

This voyage of the *Oregon* was well documented, as it was the same ship that carried official correspondence announcing California's admission to the Union. There were a number of interesting entries included in the ship's log.

The *Oregon* stopped at five other ports before reaching San Francisco. On October 5, at 1:00 a.m., the *Oregon* pushed north in heavy winds and opposing sea. Although they passed the steamer *Antelope*, the rough sea slowed them down, adding an extra thirty hours to the passage.

The *Oregon* arrived at Acapulco at 5:00 p.m. on October 8, 1850, having passed the steamer *Ecuador* just three hours earlier. The ship's journal contained another intriguing entry about the passengers aboard the *Cremona:* they were abandoned at Acapulco to fend for themselves when their ship was condemned.

The *Oregon* pushed out to sea at 1:00 p.m. on October 9 and arrived in San Diego on the 16th. The Captain's logbook recorded another piece of information gleaned in San Diego. It told of sickness in the shipping lanes and cholera at San Blas (islands off Panama).

On October 17, the *Oregon* entered the Santa Barbara Channel and faced headwinds into Monterey, where they arrived at 2:00 a.m. the following day. After a short stop, the ship was moored to the dock, loaded with mail and supplies, and then pushed north to San Francisco.

The steam ship *Oregon* was ceremoniously decorated from maintop to stern rail as it pulled into San Francisco Bay. After a fast seventeen-day passage from Panama, the excited travelers lined the rail as the entrance of the bay came into view.

On Friday, October 18, 1850, all one hundred and sixty-nine passengers and crew aboard the gallant steamer *Oregon* were welcomed into San Francisco harbor with cheers from all who had gathered. Many ships lay at anchor in anticipation of *Oregon's* arrival under the command of Captain Patterson.

The ship brought the official dispatch of California's admittance to the Union. Spectators and dignitaries hailed the thirty-first state of the union with guns and cannon fire. Capitan Harrison of the *Bark Novelty* out of Liverpool ordered the first guns fired. The stars and stripes flew from every mast in the harbor, as Isaac's ship proceeded to Sausalito, where the passengers went ashore.

Steamboats made daily trips up the delta from San Francisco to Sacramento, where river passage could be secured to mining camps in the gold region. At every terminus supplies could be purchased, including mules, horses, and oxen for travel to the Sierra Nevada and Northern California goldfields.

Josiah awaited Isaac's arrival at Shasta, the busy town where the wagons stopped and mule packing began. Shasta was California's northernmost station that stored and sold supplies to those trekking to the mines including those on the Trinity, Scott, Klamath, and Salmon Rivers. The trails were rugged, narrow, and often not marked. Wagons and oxen were regularly traded for mules, as the pack animals were more sure-footed and able to carry heavy loads through thick brush on difficult paths.

SUSANVILLE

The 1850 U.S. Federal Census Shasta, California, enumerated this information on October 26, 1850:

Josiah Roop, merchant, age 35, born Maryland; J. Byington, merchant, age 17; Stephen Pennet, merchant, age 24; Elizabeth Lean and Mary Lean, both age 22; all tenants listed in dwelling #214 in Shasta City.

View of the Procession Admission Day,
Crossing the Plaza in San Francisco,
October 19, 1850
Courtesy of Library of Congress

The Roops, The Arnolds & A Girl Named Susan

3

The Lure of Gold

Shasta

Isaac arrived at Shasta on November 4, 1850, and reunited with his oldest brother, Josiah. After only a brief visit, Isaac bolted for the Scott Valley, north of Shasta, where a few months earlier prospectors had found gold. Isaac set out to search for the coarse gold and nuggets that lured many a miner that year. He traveled along the Siskiyou trail and arrived in a steep canyon a few miles from where the Scott River met the Klamath River. Josiah remained in Shasta, with his thriving mercantile business.

Isaac found the work laborious as he pan-washed in the stream. The terrain was too rugged to haul in a gold-washer or a rocker. Isaac worked the gravel with a pan and a knife, crouched at the cold water's edge in the chill of winter.

1851

On January 4, 1851, J. (Josiah) Roop reported to the *Sacramento Transcript* that his brother made four thousand dollars at the Scott River mines. It was a substantial stake for Isaac. It would allow him to establish himself sooner than he had anticipated.

With thoughts of his children in Ohio, Isaac decided to save and invest his small fortune. He departed for Shasta with his earnings and spent the early months of 1851 assisting Josiah in the trade business. Sales were impressive. On March 7 Isaac sold five hundred dollars worth of goods in one day at the mercantile. On the same evening Isaac enjoyed the company of some men from Ashland, Ohio, as they played a game of horseshoes.

One evening early in the spring of 1851, a tragedy at the Oak Bottom House made headlines in the *Sacramento Transcript* newspaper. A miner was shot and killed after an argument with his partner that began during a card game. Immediately following the incident, the citizens of Shasta selected a jury of twelve men to try the case before the people. Josiah Roop was appointed as one of the jurors.

The first witness called was Isaac Roop. Isaac had followed the mining partners to their tent. He testified that, indeed, the two miners had been playing cards and were inebriated. He stated that an argument had ensued and one miner shot the other and killed him. Isaac told the jurors that he saw the accused pull a gun from his baggage and fire a shot at his partner. The bullet hit the fellow in the chest, below the left shoulder, and killed him instantly.

The accused was found guilty and sentenced to hang. That deed was carried out an hour after sentencing.

In June of 1851 Isaac traveled to Sacramento and was installed in the Masonic Fraternity. It was not long before gold fever struck him again. He left for Bear River, where he planned to spend the fall and winter doing a bit of prospecting. Isaac assured Josiah he would return in the springtime.

Josiah purchased the Oak Bottom House from John Howell. On September 8, 1851, he signed a promissory note for twenty-eight hundred dollars. Located nine miles west of the town of Shasta, the land and establishment was situated on Clear Creek. Oak Bottom served as an overnight stage stop, hotel, and saloon near Boulder Creek, between Whiskeytown and Tower House, (now situated below the waters of Whiskeytown Lake). The miners, who frequented Josiah's establishment played cards, consumed liquor, and were eager to spend their gold dust and nuggets.

On December 4, 1851, Shasta miners wrote to the editors of the *Sacramento Daily Union* about problems they had with mail delivery and the resignation of the postmaster. They reported that the Taylor Stage from Sacramento had tossed mailbags containing four hundred letters stamped for Shasta off the stage. The stage drivers' complaint was that the pay they received for mail transport was inadequate.

Their grievance was resolved when the letters were recovered, and Josiah Roop was appointed as Shasta's postmaster.

1852

In March of 1852, after a year and half of wanderlust, Isaac established himself as a permanent citizen in Shasta. Josiah was then the proprietor of the Oak Bottom House and the Old Dominion House*. He also owned a house and a lot in town. It was not long before Isaac and Josiah had amassed a sizable amount of assets in properties, merchandise, and trade goods.

Both brothers were homesick and occasionally received welcome news from family and friends in Ohio. A letter arrived by mail with news that two additional Roop brothers—Ephraim and Jonas—planned to journey overland and would join them in Shasta by the end of summer 1852.

Across the Plains

Ephraim and Jonas Roop

On March 18, 1852, Ephraim and Jonas Roop joined the Dorland Company at Rowsburg, Ohio. The group of one hundred and one Ashland and Wayne County men set out, under the command of Garret Dorland, for the goldfields in California. Their journey began when they boarded a train in Wooster. Two days later, on March 20, they were headed east on the Pennsylvania and Ohio Railroad from Massillon, Ohio, to Rochester, Pennsylvania. The group stayed in the city of Rochester, located on the Ohio River, and waited for their steamboat.

* See Appendix A

SUSANVILLE

Ephraim and Jonas boarded the steamer *Statesman* on March 24, 1852 with the Dorland party. The next day, after stops at Wheeling and Marietta, the men went ashore at Parkersburg, Virginia, located at the mouth of the Little Kanawha River. They arrived at Cincinnati on the 26th after a stopover at Portsmouth on the northern banks of the Ohio River. The group continued down the Ohio River and passed into the current of the Mississippi River on March 29.

The Dorland Company arrived at St. Louis, Missouri, on March 31, 1852, to the welcome sight of apple trees in full bloom. The men spent several days in St. Louis. April 3 was particularly eventful. As they walked through town, the men passed the courthouse, where they were witness to a slave auction. As they moved through the crowd that had gathered to watch, five black men were sold.

After returning to the waterfront the same evening, they were again stunned by the sight of the steamer *Glencoe* on fire. The explosion had killed many on board, and they watched as the ship floated down the levy in flames.

On April 4, the emigrants were glad to depart St. Louis on the steamer *St. Arge*, bound for Independence, Missouri.

The men spent a month in Independence preparing for the overland journey. They camped in tents and spent their days hunting, fishing, and stocking up on supplies for the four-month overland journey.

When the day for departure arrived, the party was hindered by the loss of several cattle. After a three-day delay, the cattle were rounded up, and Ephraim and Jonas Roop bid farewell to their old campsite at Independence. On May 8, 1852 the wagons started for the plains, and by mid-afternoon they had crossed the Big Blue River. There the travelers made camp in Indian Territory after dark.

Isaac and Josiah Roop in Shasta

In Shasta, Isaac and Josiah, along with most of the town merchants, met with William Nobles in the spring of 1852.

Nobles proposed that for a fee of two thousand dollars, he would disclose the route of the new cutoff trail he had blazed west from the Humboldt River. He explained that the new wagon road followed an easier assent and a lower pass over the Sierra. The Nobles Trail would direct emigrants precisely into the heart of Shasta's thriving town.

Nobles described how his trail left the Applegate in the Black Rock Desert near Rabbit Hole Springs, which was located just past Lassen Meadows at the Humboldt River. He told them that when the Nobles Trail departed the Applegate Trail, the route steered west and passed through the Honey Lake Valley.

In contrast, the Applegate Trail continued northwest over Fandango Pass into the Willamette Valley of Oregon. And the California Trail followed the Humboldt River southwest through the Forty Mile Desert, and then over the lofty Sierra Nevada.

Nobles explained to the Shasta citizens that the route through Honey Lake Valley was the easier path for both the emigrants and their stock. He told them that grass and water were plentiful on his route, and the wagon road made an easy climb over the Sierra. Nobles described how the emigrants would pass just north of Mount Lassen then proceed into the town of Shasta.

The Shasta citizens traveled with Nobles and made a thorough survey of the route. They set out by pack train, and traveled the three hundred miles to the Humboldt River, returning to Shasta in three weeks time. They all agreed that Nobles had fulfilled his end of the bargain; the route was exactly as he had described it: an easier pass over the Sierra.

The first immigrants began to arrive at Shasta late in the summer of 1852 via the new route. Initially there were complaints that Nobles Trail was not easily identifiable, and the terrain was rough. Although as more wagons passed over it, the route became easier to follow. The emigrants and their wagons, drawn by horse, mule and ox teams, continued to arrive at Shasta, much to the delight of the local merchants.

Josiah Prepares to Travel Back East

On March 5, 1852, Josiah Roop sold the Oak Bottom Establishment for $912 in preparation for a trip east. A couple months later, on May 8, 1852, he appointed his brother, Isaac, his legal agent, and set out from Shasta for San Francisco. It had been nearly three years since Josiah had left his wife, Elizabeth Shafer Roop, and their children, Charles age 8, Sarah 6, Mary 3, and baby Joseph 1 year old, in

Scipio Township in Seneca County, Ohio. Elizabeth had taken in boarders to help with the homestead while Josiah was away (Lucy Jackson, age 30, Emiline Denrick, 20, Catherine Sage, 19, Rosaana Hess, 17, and Lori Bloomer, 14).

Josiah was excited to embark on his first steam ship passage and thrilled that he would be returning home a wealthier man.

Isaac was a bit sad when he bid farewell to his brother, but happy in the knowledge that Josiah would soon see his family. Isaac often thought of his own children, Susan, John, and Isaiah, whom he had not seen in two years. He vowed that when he returned home, he would be a prosperous man.

Nicaragua

Josiah traveled with a group of distinguished Shasta citizens who sailed out of San Francisco on Tuesday, May 18, 1852. The men boarded the *Pacific* on a pleasant spring day, bound for San Juan del Sur, Nicaragua. The sidewheel steam schooner was referred to as an "express" transport, due to its speed on the water.

The Nicaraguan route was six hundred miles shorter by sea, and two days faster than booking passage across Panama. Even so, the route through Nicaragua would be long and wearisome. Josiah and his friends chose the cheaper, quicker passage, convinced that the earlier arrival in the East would make the trip tolerable.

When they arrived in Nicaragua, the ship's

passengers then embarked on a two hundred seventy-eight mile long adventure across the Isthmus. The men hired a horse and buggy to transport them through the rainforest, then they caught a boat across Lake Nicaragua, and finally traveled up the San Juan River to the harbor at San Juan de Nicaragua.

The trip was not an easy one, and after a week in the humid tropical jungle, Josiah became quite ill. With the assistance of his companions, he wearily made it to the bay, where the travelers spotted the blue waters of the Caribbean and their New York bound ship, *Prometheus*, at anchor.

Isaac in Shasta During That Same Time

In Josiah's absence, Isaac attended to their properties and investments in Shasta. As he was then the assistant postmaster in Shasta, he took a few days leave in May, and traveled to the postmaster's convention in San Francisco.

Ephraim and Jonas On the Trail

On May 18, the same day that Josiah departed from San Francisco, the Dorland Company experienced a welcomed monotonous day on the trail as they passed through Pawnee Territory.* The

---

* George King traveled west with the Dorland party and documented their journey in The Gold Rush Diary of G.W. King. After crossing the plains, he stayed in Salt Lake City, too sick to travel on. The train continued on without him.

previous day had been an eventful one, as the group ferried their wagons across the Kansas River. One boat sank, but luckily no lives were lost. It took the entire day to transport all the passengers across the river and to retrieve their belongings. The wet, hungry, tired, and nearly drowned travelers set camp at sunset.

Rising early in the morning, some of the men climbed a nearby hill where they observed a procession of Indians riding their ponies along the Kansas River trail. The Dorland group crossed the Vermillion River the next day, making good time on the trail that was lined with green milkweed.

Ephraim and Jonas Roop observed many graves along the route. Sickness had claimed the lives of young and old alike. They passed many other travelers, and were stunned to see one young man walking his black cow—his only companion—all the way to California.[*]

The Roop brothers hunted and fished when the opportunity presented itself, adding their catch to supplement their meager diet. The rain on the trail was not as welcome as it was on their fields back home in Ohio. They missed family and friends, and remembered how busy the days of springtime were as farmers tended to crops and livestock.

Ephraim and Jonas planned to post letters at the next fort along the trail. The emigrants would not receive news from home until they arrived in California, many months later.

On May 23, 1852 the wagon train reached the junction of the Independence and St. Joseph roads.

---

[*] The young man and his "old black cow" were seen by another traveler, many months later as they arrived in California on October 7, 1852.

SUSANVILLE

Many trains were in front of and behind them. Other emigrants warned them about illness on the trail. Homesickness and fear turned some of the travelers back toward home.

Within a week, the Dorland Party had reached the Blue River. Cholera struck the wagon train, and two poor souls were buried along the river by moonlight. The two brothers who perished were Allen and Lewis Graves from Ridgeville, Ohio. One was engaged to be married and the other had just recovered from an injury that occurred when a wagon had run him over. A day's rest was needed to tend to the sick and to collect the cattle that had busted through the corral during the night.

On June 1, 1852, the emigrants camped at the shallow and muddy, mile-wide Platte River. The next day they reached Fort Kearney. Ephraim and Jonas posted their letters and traded for supplies. One man was left at the fort, too sick with cholera to travel on.

During the next week and half, the wagon procession made good time, traveling between ten and twenty miles every day. On June 9 the train stopped to allow three men in a solitary wagon, heading east, to pass. They were a solemn and pitiful group of survivors, on their way back home. They had been a party of nine, but six of their companions had died of cholera.

On June 10 the Dorland wagon train forded the South Platte River, and pushed on, eager to put some miles behind them.

Josiah in Nicaragua

In Nicaragua, the oppressive heat of June took its toll on travelers crossing the Isthmus. The murky tepid water and the insects caused much distress to those who traveled in Central America.

On Thursday, June 10, at the end of the overland journey, a violent bout of intestinal sickness struck Josiah. His friends helped him board the ship that rested at anchor in the light blue waters of the bay. Josiah was listed among the passengers who left San Juan de Nicaragua on the *Prometheus*.

The steamer was scheduled to arrive in New York on June 21, 1852. Josiah's companions attended to him day and night, never leaving his bedside. The ship's surgeon consoled his patient, but to no avail.

On June 14, 1852, one of the most prominent citizens of northern California, died of dysentery at the age of thirty-five. Josiah Roop was buried in the Caribbean Sea about eighty miles south of Cuba.

The Overland Journey Continues

Unaware of their oldest brother's death, Jonas and Ephraim passed Chimney Rock, a well-known landmark, on June 17 as they followed the Platte River through Nebraska. The men marveled at such an unusual rock formation. They realized that in a few days they would reach the Laramie River.

The wagon train reached Fort Laramie on Sunday, June 20, where the hot and dusty travelers stopped to rest their stock and resupply. When they departed the U.S. Army trading post, they followed the North Fork of the Platte west along the sandstone bluffs in the Northern Plains. They found that the trail then became steeper and rockier as they trudged on toward South Pass in the Rocky Mountains.

Isaac in Shasta

In the first week of August 1852, Isaac was shocked when bad news arrived. He received a letter from California State Senator Royal Sprague, who had traveled on board the Prometheus with the men in the Shasta group. The letter informed Isaac of Josiah's death and burial at sea. A similar dispatch was sent to Josiah's wife along with his possessions, and an inventory of his belongings, verified by the ship's captain.

Within two years' time Isaac had lost both his wife and his brother, and was without the company of his children. His days of melancholy were broken only by the constant work required in maintaining the Shasta properties.

Josiah had owned several lots and buildings that housed the post office and the Old Dominion House on Shasta's Main Street. Isaac managed the properties, and had invested his own time and money to ensure the success of their investments. During the hot days of late summer, Isaac was appointed postmaster in Shasta. He had been employed as assistant postmaster, so the transition was an easy one.

However, to follow in Josiah's shoes was miserable, at best. Isaac kept himself busy and was an active and prominent citizen in Shasta. He was elected as Chairman during a Whig meeting held in Shasta on Saturday, August 28, 1852.

Shasta Happenings

On September 9, 1852, Jonas and Ephraim arrived at Shasta after just nine days shy of six months on the emigrant trail. The reunion with Isaac was cheerful—until they learned of Josiah's death.

Jonas quickly began practicing in his profession as a physician. He also assisted Isaac by serving as deputy postmaster in Shasta.

Ephraim lit out to do a bit of prospecting, as Isaac began plans to settle Josiah's estate.

On Tuesday, November 2, 1852, Isaac ran as a Whig candidate for the Assessor position in Shasta. The final election results tallied for Assessor were: Democrat Terbush - 863 votes, and Whig Roop - 674 votes. Although Isaac lost the election, he was not down long. His duties as postmaster kept him busy. He was also an active member of the Mason's Western Star Lodge No. 2.

Isaac attended Shasta's Probate Court in November, acting as the administrator of Josiah Roop's estate. Isaac was permitted to sell the first of Josiah's properties—a half interest in a corral located in the town of Shasta, which brought two hundred eighty dollars.*

---

* See Appendix A

SUSANVILLE

Isaac met with Luther and George Woodman to discuss the purchase of the property they owned two miles east of the town of Shasta. Isaac offered five hundred dollars for the seventy acres of land located on the Nobles Trail. They accepted his offer, and the sale was concluded after the New Year.

Flames in Shasta

On November 28, 1852, the first of two serious fires ignited in Shasta. At about 3:00 a.m., the first fire began at the Arcade Saloon on Main Street. The fire spread up the stairwell and then leaped to several buildings on the west side of the street, and the Shasta Courier building on the east side. All were a total loss. The fires were extinguished fairy quickly, due to the fast response of citizens who assisted in dousing the flames. Recent heavy rains also aided the efforts of the fire brigade.

The blaze did not approach Roop's Old Dominion House; it was spared. In March of 1853 Isaac had the Old Dominion appraised at four thousand dollars and sold Josiah's interest in the store.[*]

The second and most devastating fire occurred in Shasta on Tuesday afternoon, June 14, 1853. Flames erupted in the vacant Parker House at about four o'clock in the afternoon. The fire spread quickly and destroyed nearly the entire town of Shasta. Seventy buildings were destroyed in the business district, including every store, hotel, and saloon. Josiah owned the building that housed the post office on the north

---

* See Appendix A

side of Main Street next to the Empire Hotel. It was completely destroyed.

Isaac risked his life when he retrieved all the ledgers and mail located within the post office. He quickly piled the contents in the middle of the street, a substantial distance from the flames. There was no time for residents to save their personal belongings, as the fire spread so quickly. Amazingly, no lives were lost in the Shasta fire.

Isaac lost all of his personal possessions when the Old Dominion and all the buildings on the on the north and south side of Main Street burned to the ground. About forty buildings remained, small dwellings for the most part, and a few businesses at each end of the town. The heaviest losses in Shasta included Josiah Roop's properties, with an estimated value of four thousand dollars, and Isaac's investments of roughly ten thousand dollars.

For three years Isaac had saved, invested, and worked diligently. All that he had amassed went up in smoke. He had naught left but a small income as Shasta's postmaster, a town lot, and some acreage east of town.

Unsure of how he would proceed, Isaac buried himself in town affairs. He kept busy, which took his mind off his distress. He volunteered and was appointed school commissioner.

Town meetings commenced immediately after the fire as the citizens made plans to grade and widen Shasta's Main Street. Their strategy, they believed, would prevent any future fires from jumping from one side of the street to the other.

SUSANVILLE

1853

On July 9, 1853, Isaac attended the Whig State Convention in Sacramento as a Shasta County delegate.

When he returned home, he began to grow tired of the hectic life in Shasta's Gold Rush town. He was dismayed by the loss of his wife and brother, as well as the most recent blow: the loss of almost everything he owned in the fire. He missed his children, and was no closer to a reunion with them. He had little to show for the three years he'd spent in Shasta. He decided on yet another life change.

Isaac knew he must explore other opportunities for financial gain. He thought of William Nobles, who had visited Shasta the previous year. He recalled Nobles' appealing description of the Honey Lake Valley. He agreed with Nobles that there was a need for an emigrant station in that location. A new trading post on the Nobles Trail would provide the opportunity Isaac needed. He decided it was time to move on and begin again.

He wrote to his children, Susan, John, and Isaiah, and told them he planned to leave Shasta and establish a trading post in Honey Lake Valley.

Ephraim and Jonas

Jonas Roop stayed in Shasta for less than a year. He bid Isaac and Ephraim farewell shortly after the fire in June of 1853, and made his way to San Francisco. He joined and quickly made acquaintances with other passengers who were departing for Ohio. Jonas arrived home in Ashland County on a hot and humid day in late July. He then assisted his family in preparation for a move to Iowa.

Ephraim remained in Shasta with Isaac, and would go with him to Honey Lake Valley.

SUSANVILLE

4

Honey Lake Valley

Roop's Trading Post

1853-1854

The weather ranged from ninety-six to one hundred degrees during the first week of August of 1853 as Isaac prepared to leave Shasta. He had resigned as postmaster, and D. Harrill was appointed to replace him. Isaac purchased two horses and set out in an easterly direction towards the Honey Lake Valley. He passed the first emigrants of the season, who were traveling along the Nobles Trail. They were headed west to Shasta and would arrive there the third week of August.

There were an astounding number of people, wagons, and animals that traveled overland in 1853. The *Marysville Herald* received information from an emigrant who had arrived in Downieville, Sierra County, on August 5, 1853. The emigrant from

Missouri estimated that some twenty thousand people would make the trek to California and Oregon during that season. He reported that, although the Humboldt River was flowing high, grass for livestock was declining. It was difficult for those who traveled west on the California Trail as they crossed the Forty Mile Desert. In contrast, emigrants who came over the Nobles Trail found plenty of water and feed for their animals.

Isaac arrived in the Honey Lake Valley early in September of 1853. He selected the ideal site for a trading post, located in a grassy meadow along the banks of Smith Creek. He posted a notice claiming all the land for two miles along the Susan River, from the bluff and timberline, and east to the upper end of the valley. Centered in the stretch of land Isaac selected, sat the scenic meadow and creek where he planned to build his emigrant station.

Isaac spent the early months of fall tending his land claim, and exploring the high desert terrain in the Great Basin. He traveled along Nobles Trail and established a friendly rapport with Chief Winnemucca of the Northern Paiute tribe, who had a camp near Pyramid Lake.

Isaac returned to Shasta in November of 1853 and planned to spend the winter there. When he arrived he noticed that the citizens were busy putting up new brick buildings that stood side by side along Shasta's main street.

While he was in Shasta, Isaac attended to his own business affairs and finalized Josiah's estate.* As Josiah had died without a will, the burden fell upon Isaac's shoulders as his agent to wrap up his brother's

---

* See Appendix A

business matters. Isaac had sold Josiah's house and lot in Shasta earlier in the year for two thousand dollars. He met with the buyers regarding the payment that was due. Isaac secured the funds from the sale of Josiah's properties for his brother's wife and children.

On January 17, 1854 Isaac sold the town lot he owned in Shasta for five hundred dollars.

In the early summer months of 1854, Isaac, Ephraim, and companions, William Weatherlow and William McNaull, loaded a wagon full of supplies in Shasta and tracked along the Nobles Trail to the Honey Lake Valley.

Early in life, both Isaac and Ephraim had learned the principles of farming and building. They wasted no time in planting a garden and also began to build a log structure. Theirs would be the first trading post in the Honey Lake Valley, which was then considered part of the Utah Territory.

Referred to as Roop House and Roop's Trading Post, the log cabin measured nineteen feet by twenty-eight feet. The space between the logs was chinked to keep out the weather, and the floor was dirt. A stone fireplace was constructed on the south wall that allowed the afternoon sun to warm the stones, which in turn, warmed the interior of the building. The door and window were located on the east side of the building. Bark was saved when they stripped the logs, and was used as siding on the gable ends.

The Roop brothers were hard at work building the cabin when Lieutenant E.G. Beckwith greeted them. Beckwith was exploring the Nobles Trail on assignment to locate possible routes for a transcontinental railroad.

Roop House, Old Fort Roop
The roof was replaced. In this picture it presents a steeper pitch
than when it was originally built in 1854. A large portion of the
original log structure still stands today, as it was when the
trading post was built over one hundred and fifty years ago.

Courtesy of Lassen County Historical Society

The first proposed rail route west was mapped
across the Madeline Plains into Big Valley, and then
along the Pit River. The final route, which was
selected from Beckwith's railroad survey, passed
through the Truckee Meadows.

The first wagon trains of the season arrived in
the Honey Lake Valley on a midsummer's day in 1854.
Most of the emigrants who traveled the Nobles Trail
stopped at Roop's Trading Post, where they purchased
supplies and signed the register.

The leather-bound journal, known as the

SUSANVILLE

Roop House Register, recorded the date of arrival, the emigrant's hometown, their destination, as well as the number of wagons, people, and stock. Isaac also posted entries in the log, which contained opinions, gossip, and witty reflections about daily activities.

Isaac frequently traveled back and forth between Shasta and the Honey Lake Valley, promoting Nobles Trail and his new emigrant station.

During the first few years after the trading post was established, Isaac spent the cold winter months in Shasta. In November of 1854, the probate court in Shasta County approved the final settlement of Josiah's estate. Isaac attended the settlement hearing of his brother's estate.

Five Years Parted

1855

The year 1855 marked five years since Isaac had sailed for California. He had not returned to Ohio to see his children, and he missed them dearly. Susan had reached the age of fourteen, John was twelve, and Isaiah was ten years old. All of Isaac's children had just celebrated their birthdays the past November.

Isaac's parents and several of his younger siblings, as well as close family friends, planned to move to Iowa. The promise of cheap and fertile lands in Iowa drew farmers west out of Ohio, where land prices had steadily increased. The climate and long growing season lured farmers to Iowa, where the crops flourished in the wet spring and warm summer months. The Roops planned to move to Keokuk County, located fifty miles west of the Mississippi River on Iowa's eastern border. Joseph and Susannah Roop intended to take Isaac's middle child, John to Iowa with them.

Susan was firm in her decision to stay in Ohio with her Gardner grandparents until the time she hoped she could join her father in California. She understood the necessity of remaining in a stable home, and did not want to leave the grandparents who cherished her. She knew her father could offer little in the way of creature comforts; he lived in a log cabin filled with trading supplies. Isaac could not provide the necessities a young girl needed, and the living conditions in the Honey Lake Valley were rustic at best. Susan enjoyed a safe and comfortable life in Ohio that included school, church, and friends.

Safety was another consideration. Isaac did not want to risk the lives of his children by bringing them to an unsettled region. In the 1850s, California was teaming with travelers, marauders, and miners down on their luck. When the surface gold ran out, many miners who remained in California abandoned the creeks and canyons, looking for new sources of income. Some returned home, but many—particularly those who had spent every last speck of gold on drink and gambling—roamed the countryside in search of legal and, in some cases, illegal opportunities.

It would take many years of hard work and many new settlers to tame Roop's town. Isaac understood that the best place for his children continued to be with his family.

SUSANVILLE

Isaac posted a letter to his daughter[*]:

Miss Susan E. Roop
Shasta Cal June 5ᵗʰ 1855

Dearest and Loved Daughter
I have today received a letter from your uncle John Gardner and was glad to hear that you and all was well but I must confes that I was sadle disappointed for I expected to get a letter from you this mail but to non came well I will get one the next mail
you uncle John wrote me that he thought that you all was a going to Iowa next fall. Think that you had better come to this Country I know that it would be the best thing you all could do but be it as you all thinks but I hope to go home this fall and shall if all you might for Dearest Daughter I have now been away from you and your Loved Brothers to long already much longer than I like but I have not received my money for that Masonic Hall yet and what I had left after the fire I have put in to my farm so I am strapped and
should you all move to Iowa before I get back you must make such disposition with my things as you think best my furniture you had better sell but the bedding, books. I would

---

[*] This letter is presented with spelling and punctuation exactly as Isaac wrote it.

rather if you want keep them and by no means part with any of your Mothers Clothing. Keep them all except such things of them as you may wish to give to her Sisters Tell your Grand Mother to do as she may think best If she thinks but sell all except Bed Clothes, Books and such clothing of your Mothers and by no means part with Those - however Loved Daughter you are to consult your own feelings in this matter.

If you go out to Iowa will Isaiah go with you? O how I would love to see you and your Brothers and all once more but I must abide my time. All is for the better I hope. Do you go to school steady and do you learn fast are questions I often think of - I heard from you and Isaiah last week by Aron Markleys son he left Ashland sometime in April he said that he seen you at a party. Just a night or two before he left he said that you was well and hearty and Isaiah was fat as he could be and you was about grown up busy from... do you wash Sallet now with a cloth eh) Ask your Aunt Kate if she puts young goslings to roast as usual. on the hug racks but enough of this nonsense.

Why don't you write to me oftener. I think you might write at least once every month for I want to hear from you often and all see how you improve in Writing your Uncle

SUSANVILLE

Ephraim is still with McNaull and doing well. I sent you my likeness some time ago did you get it was takeing in long frame standing with my Masonic Dress on in the Royal Arch Degree. I hope you have received it-

What has be come of Samuel--as he has not written to me for some time. I think you all have about forgotten me We intend to have Celebration (Masonic) on the 25th day of June. I wish you could be here on that day. Can't you stop over in the evening of some fine Sunday and pay me visit

how is your Grand Parents health this Summer is it good? do you go up to Ashland and see your little Brother often. O how I wish that you was all out here how I would like it.

The mail is about closeing no more at - I shall write the next mail yours -
(unreadable) *until death*

The Roops, The Arnolds & A Girl Named Susan

5

Settlers

Keokuk County, Iowa

1856

The Roops

In 1856 Isaac's parents, Joseph and Susannah Roop, were among a group of Ashland County, Ohio, residents who relocated to Keokuk County, Iowa. The Roop's new homestead was situated in Jackson Township, located in southeast Iowa just east of Rock Creek and south of the Skunk River.

The group traveled some six hundred miles from Ohio through Indiana and Illinois. They crossed Iowa's eastern border—the Mississippi River—and found a land of rolling prairie that was covered with rich soil and abundant grasses fit for grazing. Susan's brother, John also made the trek from Iowa with his grandparents and settled with them on a large farm, where they lived together with family and close friends. Susan's uncle, John Roop, his wife, Delilah, and their children established a farm near the Joseph Roop property.

The 1856 Iowa State Census Jackson, Keokuk, Iowa, showed residents:

> Joseph Roop, farmer age 63; Susannah Roop, age 62; Elizabeth Roop, age 23; Joseph N. Roop, age 20; Jonas E. Roop, physician, age 28; Margaret Roop, age 21; George Roop, age 1; James M. Wood, laborer, age 21; Mary Wood, age 24 John V. Roop, age 12.

It included these details regarding the Joseph Roop farm:

> 5 acres in corn
> 48 acres in potatoes
> 8 hogs

The Sheridans

Joseph and Susannah's neighbors and friends, Paul and Margaret Sheridan, also came to Iowa from Ashland County, Ohio. They were the same friends who took young John Roop into their home in 1850, after Isaac's wife died and he set out for California.

SUSANVILLE

James Gardner also traveled to Iowa with the Sheridans, and lived with them for a short time until he could get settled on his own. James Gardner was Susan Roop's uncle, her mother's younger brother. They were raised together and James was much like a brother to Susan, as was his younger brother, Thomas Gardner.

Thomas moved to Iowa by 1860 and moved in with the Sheridan family after James moved out.

The details of the Sheridan family (notated with various spellings in the following census documents) as listed in the 1856 Iowa State Census Jackson, Keokuk, Iowa are:

> Paul Sherraden, farmer, age 33; Margaret Sherraden, age 32; George Sherraden, age 8; James Gardner, blacksmith, age 24.

Four years later, the 1860 U. S. Federal Census Jackson, Keokuk, Iowa gives these details:

> Paul Sheraden, farmer, age 35; Margaret Sheraden, age 34; George Sheraden, age 11; Thomas Gardner, wagon maker, age 22.

John Roop

John Roop, the sixth son born to Joseph and Susannah Roop, was the first of his family to settle in

Iowa. He moved west in 1848. His picturesque farm included a fine residence and a large barn situated on three hundred acres in Jackson Township near Richland, Iowa. John was known for his perseverance and brawn, which aided him in the building of his respectable homestead. He had previously sold a farm in Jefferson County, which provided the funds to finish his Keokuk County residence.

John's first marriage was to Elizabeth Sheridan, on November 26, 1846 in Ohio. They had two children, Susan E. Roop and John F. Roop. Elizabeth died in childbirth on March 15, 1850, two years after they arrived in Iowa, leaving John a widower. Their baby, John F. Roop, age 4 months, died on July 1, 1850. Both mother and baby were buried in Friends Cemetery, Richland, Keokuk County, Iowa.

A similar fate struck his older brother, Isaac, who lost his own wife, Nancy, to typhoid fever just two months later in May of that same year.

John was married a second time, on November 6, 1852, to Delilah Broiliar. Together they had six children: Joseph W. Roop, Mary A. Roop, Martha F. Roop, Arthur W. Roop, Walter D. Roop, and the youngest, Grant Roop, who died young.

Here are the details listed in the 1856 Iowa State Census Jefferson County, Iowa:

> John Roop, farmer, age 28; Delila [Delilah] Roop, age 25; Susan E. Roop, age 8; Joseph W. Roop, age 3; Mary Roop, age 1.

SUSANVILLE

The details of the John Roop farm were:

6 acres oats 140 bushels
25 acres corn 1200 bushels
1 acre potatoes 125 bushels
22 hogs value, $135

By 1860 the Roops were well settled in Jackson Township, Keokuk County, Iowa. The John Roop farm was located in Section 13. The post office was fixed at Ioka.

John's parents, Joseph and Susannah, lived nearby, as did the Paul Sheridan family. By 1870 Joshua White, his wife Catherine, and children, Mary and David, established a farm in Section 34 of Jackson Township. The Whites were the same close friends who had taken Isaiah Roop into their home after his mother, Nancy, died.

Honey Lake Valley

Nobles Trail

In the spring of 1856, settlers began to stream into the Honey Lake Valley seeking unclaimed land that remained in the rural areas of California. Many of the early landowners spent their first few years working the land. They built shelters in the summer, and departed over the mountains to the lower valleys in the winter.

On April 26, 1856, Honey Lake Valley residents met at Roop's cabin to create and proclaim a new territory and establish its boundaries. The meeting was organized by Isaac Roop and Peter Lassen. Twenty men approved twenty laws for the new territory of Nataqua, which encompassed a vast portion of western Utah Territory.

In their haste to define the boundaries, the men were apparently unaware that the territory they had created did not include Rooptown and other areas of Honey Lake Valley. They were satisfied in the knowledge that the new territory politically separated them from California and the Utah Territory.

In August, Isaac planned to leave for Shasta. It would be the last year that he would leave the trading post during wintertime. Just before his departure four large wagon trains arrived that intended to winter in the Honey Lake Valley.

The families in those groups had crossed the Sierra earlier in the season, and returned to Honey Lake Valley to settle in the area. They reported to Isaac that gold diggings were active near Rabbit Hole Springs and Antelope Springs, located along the Nobles Trail in the Black Rock Desert.

After Isaac arrived in Shasta he delivered a dispatch to the *Shasta Republican*. The October 25, 1856 edition of the newspaper printed Isaac's report on summer activities in the Honey Lake Valley. In it he stated that pioneers were quickly building homes and improving their ranches, and that he had counted forty-five settlers in the valley. He also reported that during the summer of 1856, the Honey Lake Valley was filled with abundant grass, and crops were plentiful.

Isaac's report to the newspaper included confirmation that the emigrants were well pleased with Nobles route, as there was plenty of water and grass for the animals. The emigrants reported that grass was scarce on the Carson route. Many trains had turned back after arriving at the Humboldt Sink, and had retreated to join the Nobles Trail.

The emigrant wagons on the Noble's Trail meandered over dusty roads, passing through sagebrush, greasewood, and juniper that covered the Great Basin. It was home to abundant wildlife including sage grouse, jackrabbit, pronghorn, and mule deer.

Once the emigrants passed through the Smoke Creek Desert, they approached the Honey Lake Valley, leaving the desert behind when they arrived at the tree line near Roop's trading post.

Isaac recorded the number of emigrants and livestock journeying on the Nobles road during the 1856 season as:

123 - wagons
613 - men
114 - women
159 - children
8,564 - cattle
350 - horses
3,700 - sheep

1857

In the spring of 1857 Isaac left Shasta and headed home to the Honey Lake Valley, following Nobles Trail. He transported enough supplies to begin construction of a sawmill on the Susan River at the base of mountains that were heavily timbered with pine, fir, and cedar trees. Willow and cottonwood trees also grew along the rivers and streams leading into Rooptown.

After a stopover at Hat Creek Station, he reached Feather Lake, and Isaac knew he was close to home.

Wayne County, Ohio

In the summer of 1857, when Susan Roop was fifteen, she moved with her grandparents to Wayne County, Ohio. The area where they settled was in the small village of Jackson, also referred to as Old Hickory. It was located in the northern part of Wayne County, about twenty-five miles east of their former home in Ashland County.

Susan's grandfather, John Gardner, purchased Lot No. 1 from James Smith on June 30, 1857. The home and property he purchased was located on the northeast side of Main Street in Jackson, one of five villages in Canaan Township.

As fall approached John and Jane Gardner, along with sons, John, James, David, and granddaughter Susan, were comfortably settled in their new home.

Susan's grandfather then purchased Lot No. 32 from John and Elizabeth Blocker on the southwest side of Main Street, where they planned to open a wagon shop. John and his sons were respected wagon makers, who established their business in a prime location in town.

SUSANVILLE

The men built and repaired wagons, spending much of their time repairing wheels. In their profession, they were referred to as wainwrights or wheelwrights.

Wooden wagon wheels required constant attention, as there was a good deal of stress placed upon the wheels when the wagons—filled with goods and supplies—passed over rough roads. The wooden parts of the wheel could shrink in the hot sun, causing a break or parts to fall off. The Gardners repaired and returned the road-ready wagons to their customers in good time.

Susan attended school in a one-room schoolhouse not far from where she lived in Jackson Village. On November 13, 1857, she celebrated her sixteenth birthday.

Susan's brother, Isaiah remained in Ashland County, and saw his sister occasionally. Neither Isaiah nor Susan had seen their brother, John, since he left for Iowa the previous year. The three Roop children had not seen their father in seven years.

Roop's Sawmill
Courtesy of Lassen County Historical Society

SUSANVILLE

6

Nevada Territory

Susanville

1857-1858

Isaac spent the summer of 1857 energetically building his sawmill. He also spent time at the trading post. In the evening hours he studied law.[*]

Emigrants continued to arrive in Rooptown by way of Nobles Trail. Isaac regularly sent correspondence, to the *Shasta Republican Newspaper* in which he shared the goings-on in the Honey Lake Valley.[†] Other publications picked up the news, as did the *Marysville Daily Herald* of June 15, 1857. They quoted Isaac in the column titled "The Rains and the Crops at Honey Lake": *We had a glorious rain yesterday—one of our regular old American thunderstorms.*

---

[*] Isaac's spectacles are on display at the Lassen County Historical Museum in Susanville, CA.

[†] Newspapers published information received from correspondents who lived in remote settlement areas. Isaac Roop regularly sent in the latest news, such as "Letter from Honey Lake" and "Letter from Nevada Territory."

Rooptown was growing rapidly. A dozen homes were under construction, and Isaac made the observation that the pioneers were industrious and good-natured people.

The ranchers were busy fencing and planting their acreage, and many claimed a section of land. A majority of the early settlers were in favor of reducing the size of the ranch properties to one hundred and sixty acres each. A portion of the valley land was planted, and the crops were doing well. Many crops were harvested during the year, including bushels of wheat, corn, potatoes, and other vegetables.

The miners in the area reported to Isaac that they were able to make two to five dollars a day prospecting for gold. The miners who owned land in the Honey Lake Valley spent the summer months improving their property.

Roop's sawmill was completed in August of 1857. The first boards produced at the mill were sawn timber of pine, fir, and cedar. Isaac also finished constructing a blacksmith's shop and a coal pit during that same year. Ten years after completion of Roop's mill, there were seven mills operating in the Honey Lake Valley.

Another early settler, and one of Isaac Roops neighbors, Cutler Arnold, completed the first hostelry and eatery on the northeast corner of the present-day Main and Union streets. Referred to as Cutler Arnold's (Log) Hotel, it was the first hotel in Rooptown. Measuring one and one half stories high, the building was constructed of hewn logs. At the time it was built, it served as the only public hotel and dining service in town.

SUSANVILLE

Alexander Arnold, Cutler's younger brother joined him in the valley, moving from Sierra County where he was employed as a teamster, miner, and trader. Alexander settled in Cutler's hotel, although it was limited in space as merchandise filled the cramped quarters.

Travelers who stopped there discovered that a hardy meal was available for purchase, but there was little space in the attic to lay a bedroll for the night.

As fall turned into winter, talks with the Indians in the Honey Lake Valley commenced. Since the arrival of settlers in the region, skirmishes occasionally occurred between the settlers and the Indians.

Colonel Thomas (T.J.) Henley, the territory's Indian Agent, appointed Isaac Roop, Peter Lassen, and Jonathan Williams as his representatives to negotiate with the Indians. Blankets and other goods were offered in exchange for peace. The articles were handed over to the Indians when the treaty was agreed upon.

As the winter snows of early 1858 melted, the sawmill in Rooptown was in full operation. The mill operated under the name of Roop, McNaull, and Company. It produced a large volume of cut lumber that sold for thirty dollars per one thousand board feet.

As new emigrants continued to settle in the valley, Isaac was actively involved in efforts to establish governance in the high desert region. In April of 1858, Roop named the town "Susanville" in honor of his only daughter, Susan.

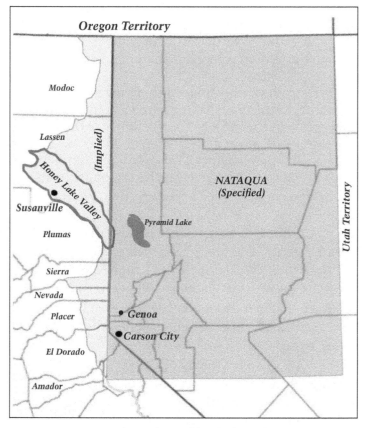

Nataqua was formed out of lands along the Eastern
Sierra and Western Utah Territory in 1856.
The portion of Nataqua located in western Utah Territory would
be declared part of the provisional Territory of Nevada in 1859.

SUSANVILLE

Early settlers, and possibly Isaac, mistakenly believed that he had also named the Susan River after his daughter. William Nobles had already named the Susan River when Isaac arrived in Honey Lake Valley in 1853. In 1852 Nobles traveled through the valley to promote a new emigrant trail, and he named the river then in honor of his wife, Susan Parker Nobles.

The farmers in the valley were glad of the spring rain and hot summer months. The soil produced abundant harvests of wheat, barley, and oats. The stock that grazed in the Honey Lake Valley were healthy and numerous. Vegetables and fruit were plentiful, and Isaac particularly enjoyed tending the fruit trees he propagated on his property.

Wagon trains continued their journey west, passing through Susanville on the Nobles Trail. The hardy emigrants followed the westward migration in search of new land and open spaces.

Provisional Governor

Approximately six months before Susanville became the official name of the town, Isaac Roop and a group of Honey Lake Valley citizens traveled to Genoa, Utah Territory, late in October of 1857. It would take four or more days in good weather to travel the hundred and thirty-mile distance on horseback.

The men met with Carson Valley representatives

to discuss territorial boundaries. The Carson Valley citizens and the Honey Lake Valley citizens together endorsed a Provisional Territory. It included the area from the Goose Creek Mountains to the east, the Sierra Nevada to the west, the Oregon and Utah line to the north, and the Colorado River to the south.

Judge Crane was appointed as delegate to petition Congress to secure the lands of the Great Basin, independent of California and the Utah Territory. There were twenty-eight men appointed at the meeting to manage the initial administration, including five from the Honey Lake Valley: Isaac Roop, Peter Lassen, Cutler Arnold, William Hill, and L. C. McMurtry.

1859-1861

On July 28, 1859 a convention of delegates met in Genoa. They agreed upon a separate territory in the Great Basin, and declared a separation from the Utah Territory. On September 7, 1859 Isaac Roop was elected Provisional Governor of the Territory of Nevada. In Genoa, which served as the Second Judicial District, Utah Territory, he was sworn in on December 13, 1859.

On December 15, 1859 Governor Roop delivered his first annual message to the legislature assembled at Carson City. He stressed that separation from the Utah Territory was essential as the citizens of the new territory desired local control to establish their own courts and county organization.

After the legislature accepted the governor's

message, the assembly proceeded to draft a petition to Congress, demanding their request be expedited.

The legislature then adjourned until the first Monday in January. Isaac attended a Christmas Ball held at the City Exchange in Carson City on Monday, December 26, 1859.

June 12, 1860 Governor Roop corresponded with Colonel F.W. (Fredrick) Lander regarding Indian hostilities in the Honey Lake Valley. Residents were panicked after Indians descended into the area and burned several homes and scattered livestock.

Lander and his troops were on expedition for the U.S. government clearing and protecting the overland wagon roads as far west as the Sierra. They had just set up camp near Honey Lake Valley to repair their wagons and rest the mules and horses. Isaac sent an urgent official dispatch to Colonel Lander requesting troops be sent in to protect citizens in the valley and travelers on the overland wagon road.

Isaac urged Lander: "As provisional Governor of Nevada Territory, I therefore call upon you, as one having the interests of the frontier citizen at heart, and as an officer of the General Government, to aid us in our extremity." *

During the month of July, 1860, Colonel Lander responded by moving fifty soldiers from the Presidio in San Francisco into the unprotected areas in the Nevada Territory. The troops arrived in two companies of twenty-five men each, one led by Captain John Byrd and the other by Captain William Weatherlow.

Several weeks after reaching a peace agreement

---

* Correspondence between Roop and Lander was published in the Daily Alta California, Thursday June 21, 1860.

with Colonel Lander, young Winnemucca, Chief of the Northern Paiutes, led his twenty-four warriors from Pyramid Lake to Susanville. There they met with Governor Roop and twenty-four prominent citizens to negotiate a settlement. Winnemucca expressed his wish to continue peaceful relations with the non-natives in the valley. After a peace pipe was passed around, an agreement was reached, all parties shook hands, and the Honey Lake Valley conflict of 1860 came to an end.

The first post office was established in Susanville on October 16, 1860, in a little building on the north side of Main Street between Lassen and Gay Streets. Isaac Roop was re-appointed postmaster. Before that time, Isaac had originally been appointed postmaster on March 17, 1859, and he had delivered the mail about town before the post office was established.

Susanville had the only post office in the area until five new postmasters and post offices were established between the years 1864-1866. They were:

Levi Breed, at Janesville in 1864
Carleton Goodrich, at Copper Vale in 1864
John Pine, at Soldier's Bridge in 1864
Charles Batterson, at Milford in 1866
Alvaro Evans, at Evan's Ranch in 1866

Isaac Roop served as the first provisional Territorial Governor of Nevada for a year and a half. On March 22, 1861, James Nye of New York was appointed Territorial Governor of Nevada.

SUSANVILLE

When he arrived in Carson City in July, Nye issued a proclamation that established the new Territory of Nevada.

The Governor called for a territorial census to be taken in 1861. Susanville reported two hundred seventy-four residents. In August an election was held to select members of the legislature. Isaac was elected to serve on the territorial council, and John Wright was elected territorial representative for the ninth district.

In Ohio

1860-1861

On November 13, 1860 Susan Roop turned nineteen years old. She continued to live in Wayne County with her grandparents, John and Jane Gardner and their youngest son, David.

The 1860 U. S. Federal Census Canaan, Wayne County Ohio record shows that those living in the Gardner household were:

> John Gardner, wagon maker, age 55;
> Jane M. Gardner, age 59; David Gardner,
> wagon maker, age 18; Susan Roop, age 18.

The value of property was listed as:

> John Gardner, value of real estate, $400,
> value of personal estate, $400

Susan's brother, John, turned seventeen on November 27, 1860. It had been four years since he'd moved to Iowa with his Roop grandparents.

John began studies for a career in the medical profession, following in the footsteps of his uncle, Jonas Roop. He attended medical college in Cincinnati, Ohio, in 1860 and 1861.

The 1860 U.S. Federal Census Jackson, Keokuk County, Iowa, gives this information about the Roops:

> Joseph Roop, age 68; Susanna [Susannah] Roop, age 66; Elizabeth Roop, age 27; Joseph [N] Roop, age 25; John Roop, age 16.

SUSANVILLE

7

Civil War Volunteers

In the East

1861

Tensions between the North and the South on issues of social, political, and economic differences escalated after the presidential election of 1860. During the months leading up to the Civil War, citizens braced for a conflict that would divide the nation.

Isaac worried about how the conflict would affect his family as the country prepared for war. He soon learned that both his sons had enlisted in support of the Union. In the summer of 1861 Isaiah Roop mustered at Columbus, Ohio, and John Roop mustered at Burlington, Iowa.

Isaiah Brian Roop, just fifteen years old, joined the Twenty Third Ohio Infantry on June 11, 1861. The regiment was organized at Camp Chase near Columbus, where training commenced. After drill was concluded, the company moved out on July 25, 1861 to Benwood, West Virginia. The soldiers were assigned to protect the Baltimore & Ohio Railroad and secure the Kanawha Valley.

Isaiah met the Confederates in a skirmish on September 10, 1861 at Carnifex Ferry, West Virginia. The greenhorn infantry of the Twenty Third Ohio were part of Rosecrans Brigade when they secured a Union victory during the opening months of the Civil War. Retaining control of the Kanawha Valley and the New River region, the Federal Army forced the Confederates to withdraw.

On November 16, Isaiah's regiment moved to Fayette Court House for the winter. The troops spent much of their time in the rugged mountains of northwest Virginia (West Virginia), where they rounded up guerrillas and patrolled the dense trails and roads. Isaiah Roop turned sixteen on November 30, 1861.

John Valentine Roop enlisted, at the age of seventeen, on July 11, 1861, and mustered on July 24 with the Seventh Iowa Infantry at Burlington, Iowa. John was a medical student and his skills could be useful in service to his country. On August 6, his regiment moved out to St. Louis, Missouri. After the soldiers were armed at Jefferson Barracks, they progressed to Ironton to proceed against forces in Missouri.

On the Missouri side of the Mississippi River, the fresh troops were tested at the Battle of Belmont on November 7, 1861. The Seventh Iowa Infantry performed well, although many of their men were killed or wounded.

SUSANVILLE

John Roop celebrated his eighteenth birthday on November 27, 1861. His regiment was assigned to the military post at Benton Barracks in St. Louis where they remained until early January of 1862.

In Nevada Territory

1861

The first regular session of the Territorial Legislative Assembly was held October 1 through November 29, 1861, in Carson City, Nevada Territory. Isaac Roop was in attendance and served on the territorial council. Ephraim Roop and his partner, Ephraim Spencer, brought forth a request before the elected representatives, applying for exclusive rights to operate a ferry on the Humboldt River.

The act to incorporate the Humboldt River Ferry Company was approved during the 1861 legislative session. Roop and Spencer were granted the sole privilege to land and deposit boats on each shore of the river, one mile in each direction, for the duration of ten years. The partners were directed to follow the prescribed laws and restrictions for licensed ferries, and were authorized to collect the following toll rates upon the river:

Crossing man on foot – 25 cents
Crossing man and horse – 50 cents
Crossing horse and carriage – 75 cents
Crossing two horses, or oxen and wagon – 75 cents
Crossing each additional span of horses or
    oxen – 50 cents

Crossing sheep or hogs each – 12.5 cents
Crossing loose stock each – 25 cents

Susan's Family in the East

1862

1862 was a stressful year for Susan and her family. As the new year began, Susan's brothers were still at war. John was on a mission up the Tennessee River, and Isaiah was on the march in West Virginia. It was a difficult time for Civil War families, who missed their loved ones and worried about their safety as each battle was fought. With the menfolk gone, much of the work at home fell on the shoulders of the women, children, and the aged. Funds were scarce, and John Gardner's wagon business suffered, as did many businesses during the war.

Susan's grandparents were planning to pack up and move to Illinois, but she made no plans to move with them. She had not seen her father in twelve years, and Susan was weary of waiting. She finally accepted the fact that he would not return to Ohio, and she must join him in Susanville.

Susan spoke with her grandparents of her desire to move to California, and with their support, she initiated plans to leave.

SUSANVILLE

Roop Residence Main Street Susanville
Built in 1862
Pictured Left to Right is Harry Thompson, F.V. Burris
Courtesy of Lassen County Historical Society

Susanville

1862

Harry Thompson had purchased several lots from Isaac, and had built a house on Susanville's Main Street. After the house was finished, Thompson was unable to pay for the properties he had purchased. Isaac repossessed the house, in payment.

Isaac moved into the new house, which was one of the nicest homes in Susanville. The Roop residence was established in Susanville in 1862. Isaac made plans to bring Susan out West.

Isaac attended the thirteenth session of the California Legislature in March of 1862. The meeting of both branches of the governing body was moved to the federal building in San Francisco due to flooding at the state capitol in Sacramento. During the joint meeting, Governor Nye and Commissioners Roop and Ford, representing the Nevada Territory, proposed a change to the boundary line between California and the Nevada Territory. A resolution to cede the vast area east of the Sierra, including the Honey Lake Valley, to Nevada Territory's jurisdiction, was agreed upon and adopted.

At six o'clock on April 10, 1862, a select party of gentlemen celebrated the formal opening of the Russ House on Montgomery Street in San Francisco. Thirty invited guests attended a private first-class inauguration dinner, arranged by the proprietors of the superb hotel.

Nevada Territory's Governor Nye and former provisional Governor Roop were in attendance. They offered numerous toasts, gave speeches, and bestowed the highest praise on the current administration, including President Lincoln.

The Civil War

Spring and Summer 1862

John Roop

On January 15, 1862, John Roop and the Seventh Iowa Regiment moved out from St. Louis on an expedition up the Tennessee River to Fort Henry. After they took Fort Henry on February 6,

SUSANVILLE

Grant's troops controlled the Tennessee River. They marched overland, east along muddy roads toward Fort Donelson. The Union capture of Fort Donelson on February 16, 1862, opened the Cumberland River for transport of vital supplies.

John and the weary Union soldiers advanced to Pittsburg Landing on the Tennessee River during the month of March, as they prepared to meet the Confederates at the Battle of Shiloh.

On April 7, 1862, the numbers of lives that were lost overshadowed the Union victory at Shiloh. The Union troops, under command of Major General Grant, left the terrible battle in southwestern Tennessee behind, and advanced into Northern Mississippi.

The soldiers spent the months of April and May in Mississippi, where they secured the vital Mobile and Ohio Railroad center. John Roop and the soldiers of the Army of the Tennessee joined the armies of the Ohio and Mississippi at the siege of Corinth between April 29 and May 30, 1862.

Isaiah Roop

Isaiah Roop and the Twenty Third Ohio Infantry marched through the Narrows of New River and advanced on Princeton, West Virginia, in the spring of 1862. In May they reached Giles Court House, which was located near the vital railroad bridge at Central Depot. The soldiers were assigned to protect the Baltimore & Ohio Railroad and the surrounding area from Confederate advances.

Isaiah and his companions spent the summer months scouting in the Allegheny Mountains. They celebrated the Fourth of July at Flat Top Mountain in West Virginia.

When the troops moved out, they traveled over three hundred miles by steamer and rail to Washington, D. C., arriving there on August 24, 1862. At Washington, D.C., Isaiah's Union Regiment joined the Maryland Campaign and headed toward the worst battle of the civil war.

California

Summer 1862

During the summer of 1862, many travelers continued to pass through Susanville. The town was situated on a great thoroughfare where three main roads converged from California to the Humboldt Region and to the East. Susanville's prominence during that time was indisputable, and the settlement was a convenient stop for fatigued travelers and their stock.

In 1862 about fifty homes and a good number of merchant establishments had been built in the small town. Log construction came to an end in the early 1860s as framed buildings were erected in Susanville.

The Brannon House Hotel was built on the corner of Main and Lassen Streets. The nice establishment lured travelers to stop overnight. The first framed mercantile building was put up on Susanville's Main Street. Local residents and travelers alike enjoyed refreshment at the Black Rock Saloon on the north side of Main Street between Gay and Union Streets.

A blacksmith's shop was situated on Main Street across from the Black Rock Saloon. The Humboldt Exchange, located on the south side of Main, west of Gay Street, housed a saloon and restaurant. The Magnolia Saloon, built in 1862 on the south side of Main between Lassen and Union Streets, enjoyed a lively business that catered to whiskey drinkers and card players.

Isaac Roop was an energetic and shrewd businessman. When it came to town affairs, he not only sold his land for profit but also donated land to further the development of the settlement. Isaac donated land for a cemetery and sold land to the Methodist Episcopal Church for one dollar.

Isaac installed the first officers of the Lassen Lodge No. 149 in 1862. The Masonic Order, which was organized at Richmond District in 1861, was moved to Susanville in 1862.

Isaac planted fruit trees and built a fishpond at his home, as he prepared for Susan's arrival. He sold numerous lots in Susanville. The nineteen hundred dollars owed him was secured by promissory notes, and a small amount of cash. The money he received would help to fund Susan's trip west. Since she was the former Provisional Governor's daughter, it was customary that she would travel first class.

The Civil War

Autumn 1862

John Roop

Following their successful siege of the city on May 30, 1862, John Roop and the men of the Seventh Iowa remained in Corinth, Mississippi. They built fortifications to protect the city, which was an important transportation center.

The soldiers of the Army of the Tennessee were victorious at the Battle of Corinth on October 4. There they secured important city rail lines. The Union forces shattered the hopes of the Confederates, who were prevented in advancing north into Kentucky and Tennessee. John and his companions remained on duty at Corinth through the end of the year.

Isaiah Roop

Isaiah and the Twenty Third Ohio Infantry joined the Maryland Campaign and fought at the battle of South Mountain on September 14, 1862. Although he was slightly wounded during the conflict, Isaiah and the other soldiers moved into the hills of Sharpsburg, Maryland.

SUSANVILLE

Battle of Antietam
Courtesy of Library of Congress

Three days later, they came up against the Confederates again. In the course of the battle, forever after known as the Battle of Antietam, Private Isaiah Roop, age sixteen, was seriously wounded.

The injured and dying soldiers were laid on the ground to await their turn in the surgeon's tent. Exhausted and under-trained surgeons treated Isaiah's injuries, in the most primitive of conditions. His right arm was amputated.

Isaiah was one of over nine thousand Union soldiers who were wounded in that battle. He was fortunate to have survived the battlefield surgery, performed in filthy conditions.

Soldiers who survived such operations, were transported to hospitals behind field lines.

On October 8, 1862 the men of the Twenty Third marched out to Chambersburg, Pennsylvania. Their dead and wounded, including Isaiah, were left behind. Isaiah celebrated his seventeenth birthday on November 30 as he lay in a hospital bed and suffered alongside other injured and dying soldiers.

During the Civil War there was no official process to notify the families of injured or deceased soldiers. It could take months before the relatives knew the fate of their loved ones. Families relied on friends of the fallen, as well as nurses and hospital volunteers, to pen a letter home.

SUSANVILLE

8

The Journey West

Panama
Late in 1862

Susan Goes West

On November 13, 1862, Susan Roop celebrated her twenty first birthday and prepared for her journey to California. She settled on a travel route that would take her through Panama, one that would significantly reduce travel time. It was the same passage her father had traveled twelve years earlier in 1850.

A few days after her birthday she bid farewell to friends and family and boarded a train bound for New York City. The train station in Wooster was situated on the Pittsburg, Fort Wayne, and Chicago Rail line, located ten miles south of Susan's home in Canaan Township, Ohio.

She departed Wooster on a chilly autumn day and caught the direct route to New York on the U.S. Mail and passenger express train. She traveled east out of Ohio and soon crossed the border into Pennsylvania. The train stopped in Pittsburgh, where the passengers headed east changed trains, diverting to the Pennsylvania Central Railway. After a short stop in Altoona, the train continued on to Philadelphia, and finally ended in New York.

Susan arrived at Cortlandt Street station a bit weary but excited after the day and half trip. The weather was cold, and snow had just melted on the streets of New York. A week before Susan's arrival, snow had blanketed the entire eastern seacoast from Maine to Virginia. After she secured food and lodging, she rested a few days before her ship departed.

Far from her home in rural Ohio, Susan took in the sights and sounds of chaotic New York City. Though the Civil War battles were distanced from New York, there were visible reminders on every street she passed along. The bustling city was filled with Union supporters who flew flags and held fundraisers supporting the war effort. Troops and supplies moved through the city to and from the war, as the Army of the Potomac marched out on the offensive to Virginia.

Susan made her way to the pier at the foot of Canal Street where her ship was moored. The *Champion*, a sidewheel steamer owned by the Atlantic Mail Steamship Company, was used for passenger and mail transportation.

Susan purchased her ticket, checked her baggage through to her final destination of San Francisco, and boarded the steamer along with the

The New Iron Steamship *"Champion,"*
of the Vanderbilt Line
Courtesy of Library of Congress

other passengers. On Friday, November 21, 1862, at
11:00 a.m., the *Champion* pushed out into North
River and then put out to sea. Susan settled on board
the ship as it steamed south on the North Atlantic
current, bound for the Isthmus of Panama.

Isaac Awaits His Daughter

Nevada's Territorial Legislature convened on
November 11, 1862, with all thirteen members in
attendance. Isaac Roop represented Lake County as
a member of the council (Honey Lake Valley became

part of Lake County during the 1862 session). After the oath of allegiance and the roll call was taken, the second legislative assembly continued in session. The men assembled in a fine stone building on Carson Street, which had originally housed the Great Basin Hotel. The building had been renovated and newly furnished to aid in the comfort of the representatives.

It was quite an improvement from the previous year when the legislature met at a location two miles out of town, where they had to be transported by a train, pulled by mules along a plank rail track. The second assembly was scheduled to meet for six weeks. Isaac intended to stay on in Carson City until Susan's arrival.

On Monday November 24, 1862 ex-Governor Roop entertained the legislature with a proposal. Roop gave notice in support of a forlorn Mrs. Cornelia McKnight, who requested to divorce her polygamous husband. He shared that at the time of her marriage, she was an underage orphan who was wedded against her will.

Isaac caused quite a stir when he presented a petition that would grant divorces to all women moving into the Territory, who were married under Mormon Law. Roop was of the opinion that Mr. McKnight "could afford to spare one of his five present and prospective help mates." Isaac then introduced a bill granting the same.

On November 26, 1862 the Divorce Bill was rejected. The Nevada Legislature was strongly opposed to involvement in marital squabbles, fearful that it would set a precedence that would swamp them with divorce petitions.

SUSANVILLE

Toll road franchises, gaming licenses, and limited partnerships were among the many bills that the legislature put forward during the session and a good deal of business was put into motion each day. That is except for Thursday, November 25, when the legislature adjourned early after accepting a basket of wine delivered by Mrs. Margaret Ormsby, with her compliments.

She was the widow of Major William Ormsby who was killed in the Pyramid Lake Indian War of 1860. Mrs. Margaret Ormsby was a supporter of the territorial legislature and was an astute and respected business woman in Carson City.* She was given her own seat in the legislature for the entire session.

On Friday December 5, 1862, the Governor approved a House Bill that changed the name of Lake County to Roop County, much to the delight of Isaac.

Susan's Travel Across the Isthmus

Susan sailed to Panama during the humid, rainy month of December. The sidewheel steamer she traveled aboard was built for comfort and swift passage. It was equipped with ninety-six staterooms and three hundred eighty-eight cabins. When the iron-hulled *Champion* arrived at Aspinwall, the passengers disembarked at the pier and prepared to cross the Isthmus by train.

---

* After the death of her husband William, Margaret Ormsby purchased many properties in Carson City, including the Ormsby House Hotel where she once lived. The other properties she acquired were leased out to businesses such as restaurants, boarding houses, and saloons.

The train fare was included in the price of the ticket the passengers had purchased before they departed from New York. Deckhands unloaded the passengers' luggage and deposited it, along with the U.S. mail and freight, on the steam locomotive. The Panama Railroad, completed in 1855, offered a quick and comfortable trip across the Isthmus for travelers who journeyed between New York and California.

The Panama passage, the overland mail route, and the wagon train were all popular means of transport for travelers going west before the United States transcontinental railroad was completed in 1869. The Panama Railroad ran on hollow rails built on a narrow five-foot gauge. The train twisted up hills and down through the tropical jungle as it passed over bridges and culverts. The crooked railroad path rose to a height of three hundred feet and descended to sea level as it crossed over streams and swamps.

The train covered the forty-seven and a half mile distance between the Atlantic and Pacific Oceans in a few short hours.

The threat of malarial mosquitoes, cholera, and dysentery were ever present in the Panama jungle. The pestilent clouds of bugs and sand flies in the region were a constant menace for travelers. The train's cane bottom seats kept passengers fairly comfortable. Blinds covered the windows to keep pests out, and to help passengers stay cool.

Susan enjoyed the scenery and the view of the lush damp vegetation from the safety of the train car. Panama's weather and landscape was quite different from the icy streets of New York that she had toured a week and a half earlier.

The train was twenty-four hours behind

schedule due to heavy rains and flooding on the tracks when Susan arrived in Panama City. She and the other travelers boarded a steam tug that ferried them out to their ship moored in the bay.

Their transport was the *Orizaba*, a wooden hulled steam schooner set with twin masts. It had run the Pacific route since 1856, transporting passengers, mail, and gold. The ship was equipped with three decks, ninety-one staterooms, and space for five hundred and ninety persons in steerage.

After depositing luggage in her first class stateroom, Susan and many of the other passengers took in the view from the rail. Countless travelers, including Susan, had never seen the Pacific Ocean. For them it was a thrilling sight to see from the deck of the ship.

The *Orizaba* left Panama Bay on December 2, at 5:00 p.m., plowing the warm seawaters north to San Francisco. At 1:00 a.m. on December 4, the steamers *Constitution* and *Orizaba* exchanged signals. On December 9 at 5:30 p.m. the *Orizaba* arrived at Acapulco, where it took on fresh supplies and coal. The ship departed the same night at 3:15 a.m.

On the night of December 16, the *Orizaba* passed the *Oregon*, which had also set a course north from Mazatlán. The *Orizaba* arrived in San Francisco at 4:00 p.m. on Thursday December 18, 1862, in a bay full of ships. Under the command of W. F. Lapidge, the *Orizaba* had reached the busy San Francisco port city fifteen days and twenty-three hours after departing from Panama.

Christmas Season

1862

The *Orizaba* moored at the docks in a busy and noisy area of San Francisco where ships, cargo, and people loaded and unloaded in a flurry of activity. The wharves in the city had been extended out into the bay from city streets, where large vessels could load and unload, even at low tide. In 1850 Central Wharf had been extended two thousand feet into the bay to accommodate the Pacific Mail steamers and other large ships.

As soon as Susan and her traveling companions arrived in San Francisco, they collected their luggage and hailed a carriage to take them to the nearest hotel, which had been recommended by the ship's purser.

As heavy rain fell, Susan rested in a safe and well-situated establishment. The following day, she went to the ticket office on Broadway Wharf, and booked passage on a river steamer to Sacramento.

The California Steam Navigation Company operated daily service to and from Sacramento. The Sacramento River steamers were the conveyance of choice for many passengers traveling between San Francisco and Sacramento. With no lapse in service since the days of the Gold Rush, the paddle wheelers traveled between the two cities in nine or ten hours. The steamers stopped at landings in Benicia and Rio Vista.

The shallow draft passenger steamers, *Chrysopolis* and *Antelope*, ran the Sacramento River route on alternate days. Although Susan traveled in the cold of December, the riverboats were quite warm and comfortable inside.

The popular and luxurious *Chrysopolis* was built in 1860, with an interior that was detailed with crystal chandeliers, lush upholstery, and rosewood paneling. The glass in the cabin doors was stained in a variety of beautiful colors so that light would cast a muted glow on the interior of the rooms. Passengers enjoyed delicious food and scenic views aboard the two hundred forty five foot long vessel.

Susan disembarked at the steamer landing in Sacramento, and walked across Front Street to reserve a hotel room. The Sacramento hotels rented rooms by the day and by the week. The rate charged per day was fifty cents, and per week the price was four dollars. A delicious meal could be purchased for the reasonable fee of twenty-five cents.

It was the Christmas season and Susan enjoyed seeing the festive decorations that adorned many of the establishments. The hotels in the river city catered to the many travelers passing through.

She selected well-placed accommodations, and the clerk assured her that they would have breakfast available early in the morning in time for stage, train, and boat departures.

Although she traveled alone, Susan kept company with some of the other single and married young women who also journeyed to join their loved ones in the west. After securing a room, Susan strolled to the stage office and reserved a seat on the overland stage that would take her over the Sierra Nevada and into Carson City.

Isaac

The 1862 Nevada Legislature adjourned at midnight on Saturday, December 20. A band jubilantly led Isaac Roop and fellow representatives as they made a procession to Governor Nye's home. There the noisy revelers were invited in for a nightcap. After a late night of merriment, Isaac settled in a hotel room to await his daughter.

Newspapers printed lists of scheduled ships' arrivals into San Francisco, and also listed the names of the first class passengers. Isaac was glad to learn that Susan was in transit to San Francisco.

He soon received a wire from her at the telegraph office confirming that she would arrive in Carson City the day after Christmas. Father and daughter had not seen other in twelve years, and both impatiently anticipated their reunion

The Christmas season of 1862 was both a happy and sad time for Isaac. In a few short days he would see Susan, but he continued to worry about his sons in the war.

His youngest son, Isaiah continued to convalesce from his dreadful injury. His eldest son, John's regiment was assigned to the 1st Brigade, District of Corinth, 17th Army Corps, Department of the Tennessee.

After a skirmish at Little Bear Creek on December 12, John and the soldiers of the Seventh Iowa advanced on Forrest to hold the railroad in West Tennessee. The expedition on Forrest began on December 18, 1862 (the same day Susan arrived in San Francisco), and continued until January.

SUSANVILLE

Light snow fell during the last week of December. The roads over the Sierra Nevada were passable and in fine condition, the snow measuring only two feet at the summit. Although it made for heavy wheeling at the top, the road was packed, and the stagecoaches encountered no difficulty in traversing the mountains. Teams of men were employed at various stations to tramp down the snow, and sleighs were on hand in the event of heavy snowfall.

Susan had purchased an accommodation ticket, and left Sacramento on the stage at 6:30 a.m. Christmas Eve.

The Pioneer Stage Company was superbly outfitted with fine Concord coaches and six-horse teams. Susan traveled the Gold Rush road to Placerville. She arrived at 2:00 p.m. and stayed the night there. At 5:00 a.m. the next morning, Christmas day, the sleepy passengers climbed back into the coach and settled in the leather-bound seats, wrapped in warm coverings.

The route Susan traveled was a busy stage coach and freight road, which climbed steadily in elevation after departing from Placerville along the Pioneer Trail.

The passengers arrived at Strawberry at 3:00 p.m. where fresh snow blanketed the surroundings. Susan spent Christmas night at Strawberry Valley House. The popular resort, located some forty-two miles from Placerville, was established in the 1850s as a remount station along the Pony Express Trail. The warm and comfortable way station was adorned in Christmas garlands, and the innkeepers offered a hot meal to the travelers.

After a restful night's layover, the passengers boarded the Concord coach and left Strawberry Station at 5:00 a.m. in the dark and cold. They traveled on the Placerville-Carson Valley Road that ran south of Lake Tahoe. As the sun rose, the passengers enjoyed the views of fir and pine trees dusted with snow.

When the stage descended Carson Canyon the road was, at times, rugged and steep with hard packed snow. The road turned from snow to a mix of mud and hard packed earth as they traveled farther downhill. Descending the Carson Valley Road and approaching

Strawberry Valley Station Placerville Route,

Courtesy of Library of Congress

SUSANVILLE

the valley, they left the scenic mountains behind and proceeded through rocky open country that was covered in brush.

Susan arrived at Carson City at about 2:00 p.m. on Friday, December 26, 1862. After five weeks in transit, Susan stepped off the stage in front of the St. Charles Hotel and into the welcoming arms of her happy father. Father and daughter had a delightful reunion that was witnessed by all who had gathered at the stage stop.

The St. Charles was a spacious, first-class hotel in Carson City, which held the offices of the Pioneer Stage Company. The three-story corner building on Carson Street was a favored lodging site for state lawmakers when the legislature was in session. The location of the major stage stop enticed travelers and hotel guests alike to sit for a time in the cordial saloon on the ground floor.

After a night of rest in Carson City, Susan and Isaac caught the early afternoon stage to Virginia City. The undercarriage of the coach they traveled in was equipped with leather thorough braces, which resulted in a rocking motion that provided the travelers with a comfortable ride. They arrived in time for a late evening meal.

After the Roops reached Virginia City, the stage continued on to Salt Lake City with station stops in between.

Virginia City was a bustling boomtown, crowded with people, shops, stores, saloons, hotels, and restaurants. Isaac introduced Susan to Chief

Winnemucca who was happy to meet his friend's daughter, as he also had daughters of his own. Due to hostilities in the region, the Chief of the Paiutes recommended that the Roops spend a few extra days in Virginia City. He guaranteed a safe passage to Susanville.

Pioneer Stage Leaving Wells Fargo & Company,
C Street, Virginia City
Courtesy of Library of Congress

9

A New Home

Susanville

1863

A rich strike of silver rang in the New Year of 1863 at a mine three miles east of Virginia City. The valuable discovery caused great excitement in town as Isaac and Susan prepared to return to Carson City. People flocked to Virginia City where activity and commotion continued through the day and night.

Susan longed for a quiet place to call her own. The weather was blustery when she and her father departed for Susanville on January 4. Stagecoaches and freight wagons traveled regularly over the rough roads between Carson City and the Honey Lake Valley. There were overnight stations that catered to cold travelers and fatigued teams, located along the stage and toll roads–between Truckee Meadows and Honey Lake Valley.

Light rain fell as Susan and Isaac approached Milford, located some thirty miles southeast of Susanville. The first gristmill built in the Honey Lake Valley was situated in Milford, and there was also a hotel and saloon nearby. The trip was filled with new sights and Susan was excited to finally see the landscape that her father had written her about.

As they journeyed, Isaac commented on each settlement they passed. He was eager to show her how the valley had changed since he'd first arrived. The rugged country was filled with striking differences: tall mountains covered in trees, and spacious valleys filled with sagebrush. It was far different from the countryside she had left in Ohio.

The Roops approached Janesville, fifteen miles southeast of Susanville. The town was located at the base of the Sierra where a steam sawmill was being constructed on the creek overlooking the settlement. There were several dwellings, including a log cabin that served as the schoolhouse, a general store, a two-story lodge, a saloon, and shoe shop, as well as a blacksmith.

The carriage rolled along and came into a clearing where the settlement of Richmond stood, three and half miles south of Susanville. Located at the junction of the Diamond Mountain Road, the way station at Richmond supplied travelers and teams crossing the mountains from Quincy and Marysville. It was a popular stop for both the travelers and townsfolk, who patronized the fine two-story hotel and supply store, as well as the blacksmith and wagon shop.

SUSANVILLE

Isaac and Susan arrived in Susanville on a cold, dry winter day in that first week of January. Although the town appeared small and rustic to the young woman who had toured New York just five weeks before, Susan was joyous to see her new home. Isaac guided her past the trading post, their house, and up Main Street. He identified the homes and businesses that had been constructed since he'd first set his claim in the valley ten years earlier.

The small town was growing as new establishments and more families moved to the area. There were two blocks of buildings in Susanville when Isaac escorted Susan to her new home. There were several stores, a medicine shop, a photo gallery, a restaurant, two hotels and saloons, two livery and feed stables. A barbershop was newly established near the southwest corner of Main and Gay Streets. The first schoolhouse was built on the southwest corner of Cottage and Weatherlow Streets.

A fireproof stone building was under construction on the south side of Main Street, midway between Lassen and Gay Streets. John Hosselkus and Isaac Roop's brother, Joseph, had built the Miller and Kingsley store.

The stone building was under construction in 1863. As they knew they would finish it that year, and since the stone work is always the first to be set in a building, the year "1863" was chiseled above its entrance in the stone. The building stands to this day on Susanville's main street.

The Roops settled in a splendid home located

on the north side of Main Street, east of the Brannon House Hotel. Susan eagerly assumed the role of hostess as prominent citizens and guests came to visit her father. She relished the task of managing a home of her own. Still fondly referred to as Governor Roop, Isaac soon introduced his much-loved daughter—the town's namesake—to his friends and neighbors in the valley.

Roop County War

In January of 1863, Governor Nye appointed officers for Roop County, Nevada Territory, although Plumas County also claimed jurisdiction over the same land in the Honey Lake Valley. For several years, Plumas representatives, who ordered the Honey Lakers to pay taxes to Plumas County, had harassed the citizens in the valley. Many settlers refused to pay taxes to Plumas County since they enjoyed their independence and close association with Nevada Territory. The settlers, who were in favor of the Plumas alliance, paid their taxes to Plumas County or, in some cases, offered livestock in exchange for payment.

Susan barely had time to settle into her new home, when the recurrent boundary dispute erupted in gunfire. A rebellion broke out on Sunday morning, February 15, 1863, when Honey Lake Valley residents resisted Plumas County officials, who'd come to Susanville to collect taxes and assert their jurisdiction over Roop County.

SUSANVILLE

The conflict that occurred was referred to as the Sagebrush War and the Sagebrush Rebellion. A volley of gunfire set off the skirmish that occurred between the Plumas County Sheriff and his posse and the citizens of Roop County, who were holed up in Roop's trading post. Thereafter, the trading post was referred to as Fort Defiance and Roop's Fort.

There were over one hundred men involved in the battle as gunfire was exchanged over the course of one day. A few men suffered gunshot wounds and other injuries, but there was no loss of life.

Susan did not leave the safety of her home during the conflict, but did act as nurse tending to the injured men. Isaac acted as mediator during the day, and a truce was declared later in the evening. In the end, the residents of the valley agreed to submit to the jurisdiction of Plumas County until such time as the California Legislature granted a new county.

The merchants on Main Street in Susanville closed up shop during the conflict. Their doors opened the next morning after the truce was called. Plumas and Roop County citizens both agreed to end the fight and allow the governors of Nevada Territory and California to resolve the border issue.

After citizens of the two counties deliberated the terms of a settlement, representatives were selected from each group to pen a petition. The men retired to the Magnolia building where court was usually held and the saloon there was a favored destination. On February 16, the settlement agreement was written. Their request was then

dispatched to the governors of California and Nevada
Territory, requesting resolution.*

> *Peace Meeting*
> *A state of war existing between the authorities*
> *of Plumas County California and the authorities*
> *and Citizens of Roop County Nevada Territory*
> *a committee of Citizens of Honey Lake Valley*
> *and the leaders of the belligerent parties conven-*
> *-ed at Susan Ville for the purpose of making*
> *Some arrangements for the establishment of*
> *Peace and to stop the further Shedding of blood*
> *Frank Drake was appointed President and*
> *H.U. Jennings Secretary. Mr Pierce, Sheriff*
> *of Plumas County made the following*
> *proposition (To/wit)   Both Parties to*
> *Suspend hostilities and disband their forces*
> *he taking his men home with him, and report*
> *The case to the Governor of California reques-*
> *-ting him to confer with the Governor of*
> *Nevada Territory that the question of juirisdic-*
> *-tion may be settled peaceably – pending*
> *Such Settlement neither party to claim juris-*
> *diction, also that the citizens of the Valley*
> *Shall draw up a full Statement of the case*
> *And forever the same to the Governors of*
> *California and Nevada Territory requesting*
> *them to settle the difficulties peaceably and as*
> *Soon as possible.*

---

* The spelling, punctuation and layout exactly as was hand
written in the following document.

SUSANVILLE

Mr. Elliott thought the proposition
a fair and honorable one and thus it
would lead to a speedy Settlement of our
present difficulties. He was therefore in favor
of Mr Pierce's proposition.
Mr. Pierce (Sheriff) Moved the
Appointment of a Committee of four Cit-
-izens (two of each party) to make the state-
-ment to each of the Governors – Carried.
Mr. Elliott moved that we adopt Mr
Pierce's proposition for a Settlement
of our difficulties. Carried unanimously:
The Chairman appointed upon the
Committee of Correspondence Messrs.. Roop.
Murray. Jones & Young.
On Motion the meeting adjourned
Frank Drake Chr..
H.U. Jennings Secty..
The above proceedings is an
agreement of settlement between the contending
parties of Roop and Plumas Counties
Signed E.H. Pierce
Wm.Hill Naileigh
The above is a true & correct copy of
The proceedings of the peace meeting held in
Susanville Feb 16ᵗʰ 1863,
Wm. Hill Naileigh
Sheriff Roop County
N.T.

Invalid Corps in the East

1863

John Roop

Susan's brother, John, passed the cold winter with his regiment in a tent camp in Corinth, Mississippi. They had lost a third of their men during the engagement at Corinth in the fall of 1862. In March of 1863, the troops moved out to Bethel, Tennessee, where they remained through the spring and summer months. The soldiers were assigned to forage and scout the area, as well as guard the railroad lines in and around Bethel Station.

Isaiah Roop

Isaiah Roop recovered from the injury and amputation he'd suffered at Antietam. Although he was discharged from active service and handicapped, he was nominated by his superiors for service valor, and was assigned to the Invalid Corps.

The Invalid Corps was created in 1863 for disabled Civil War soldiers who were unfit for active field duty, due to injury or disease, but were fit for light duty. Isaiah and the other invalid soldiers were put on light duty as soon as they healed. They filled the jobs of able-bodied soldiers who were transferred to the battle lines. As the war continued, the number of soldiers who were injured, killed, and died of disease escalated at an alarming rate.

SUSANVILLE

Isaiah was assigned to the 2nd Battalion Illinois Corps at Columbus, Ohio, which had been established for soldiers whose injuries were the most serious, such as a loss of limb. Isaiah was assigned as a clerk. Other disabled soldiers worked as cooks, orderlies, and guards in the hospitals.

As the war continued, the soldiers were given work orders that included service in other military and public buildings wherever they were most needed. The name of the Invalid Corps was changed to the Veterans Reserve Corps in 1864, and was disbanded at the end of the Civil War.

Engagement

Susanville

The Second Half of 1863

The Honey Lake Valley was full of activity during the summer of 1863 as horses, mules, and oxen pulled wagons and stagecoaches over dusty roads. Hundreds of teams and people passed through Susanville on the Nobles Trail, where there was ample water and feed for the animals. After stopping for supplies, the teams headed west on Main Street.

As the travelers departed Susanville, the road quickly ascended in altitude. The emigrants enjoyed the change of scenery as they left the open desert country and entered thick forests of pine and fir. They soon came upon a clearing of grassland at Mountain Meadows where cattle grazed in the summer sun.

There, a fingerpost marked the road to Red Bluff, a route that had been recently completed.

The Sierra mountain climb on the Nobles Trail was scenic and tranquil. Although summer travel was hot and dusty, the canopy of trees shielded the emigrants from the hot sun. Twelve miles past Mountain Meadows, the wagon trains arrived at Big Meadows.* Surrounded by mountains, the valley at Big Meadows was filled with abundant grassland and streams that were lined with ash and cottonwood trees.

The north end of the Sierra Nevada range is where many of the wagon roads were linked. The Nobles, Lassen, Humbug, and Humboldt roads were among the network that extended in all directions in the vast lands of the west. Small communities sprang up along those roads as each year more and more travelers passed through.

Susan Roop set out to refine the rough frontier town named in her honor. She deplored the wickedness of saloons, and condemned the lawlessness that was prevalent in the uncultivated west. Susan had been raised in a religious home and identified herself as a Presbyterian. Although her father was raised a Dunkard,† he supported the Methodist Episcopal

---

* Today, the settlement at Big Meadows is completely submerged under the waters of Lake Almanor.
† Members of the Dunkard faith embraced Christianity and wore plain attire. They lived a simple and peaceful life, and believed in baptism by immersion. Church members held that a rich mind and service to the community was essential. Joseph and Susannah Roop were early pioneers of the Dunkard church in Ashland Ohio. Joseph N. Roop, their youngest son was a Deacon in the Ashland City Church of the Brethren (Dunkards) organized in 1879.

traditions after he moved west, as the faiths shared similar Christian values.

Susan believed it was time for the children of Susanville to be introduced to Sunday school. In June of 1863, with the assistance of Dr. Zetus Spalding, Susan taught the first religious education classes held at the schoolhouse.

The summer flew by, and Susan was content in her new home. She took pleasure in preparing family recipes using produce from the garden and fruit from the trees that her father had planted before her arrival. Peaches and apples were harvested during the season. She enjoyed baking, and often shared delicious fruit pies with family and friends. Most days, Susan kept a warmed pot of food ready, as she never turned away a hungry neighbor or visitor at her door.[*]

Isaac's work and community involvement kept him busy and away from home most days. He was active in the Masonic Lodge, he was Susanville's postmaster, and he had been admitted to the bar the previous year.

Because he had to be away from home a great deal, Isaac was concerned about the ruffians in Susanville. Susan was one of the few marriageable women in town, and Isaac feared for her safety. She was given a small derringer for protection, which she carried discreetly in her pocket.[†] Even though

---

[*] As told to Zellamae Arnold Miles by her father Medford Roop Arnold, Susan's youngest son.

[†] The gun was given to Susan by a questionable character whose name is lost to history. Susan's granddaughter Zellamae Arnold Miles was told that a man who frequented the saloons gave the derringer to Susan. The small weapon is on display at the Lassen County Historical Museum in Susanville, CA.

the town's citizens safeguarded the daughter of the former provisional Territorial Governor, Isaac requested that Susan be cautious.

The members of Lassen Lodge No. 149 were hard at work assembling a new meeting hall. Isaac occasionally dined with his fraternity brothers, and often invited them to his house for a home cooked meal.

Alexander Arnold had joined the Mason's Lodge in 1863. He assisted lodge members in the construction of the new hall, when he was not freighting out of town. He began to accept increasingly more invitations to dine at the Roop's home.

Although the food Susan served was tasty, it soon became apparent that Alexander enjoyed the company of Isaac's daughter much more than the fare.

As summer turned to fall, farmers and ranchers in the Honey Lake Valley were blessed with abundant and healthy yields during the season.

As 1863 came to a close, the winter in Susanville was a dry one. The Sierra mountain roads—usually closed due to heavy snow each year—remained open during the early winter. Four hundred rabbits from the Honey Lake Valley were delivered to market at Virginia City two days before Christmas.

A peculiar mountain fever, with symptoms of chills, headache, and dizziness, struck several Susanville citizens, who died of the ailment during the cold days of December.

Susan and Isaac celebrated her first Christmas in Susanville. Holiday festivities were modest during

SUSANVILLE

the war years, as a cloud of sadness hung over the nation. Even the snow refused to fall in December of 1863, adding to the gloom of the season for the Roops.

They received a letter from John, who informed them that he would spend Christmas in Pulaski, Tennessee, with the Seventh Iowa Volunteers. John also conveyed the news that he planned to reenlist, and would be furloughed during the month of January 1864, at which time he would return to Iowa for a visit.

By the end of the first year that Susan lived in Susanville, her friendship with Alexander had continued to grow. Although Alexander also hailed from Ohio, they did-not meet until fate brought them together in Susanville.

After winning approval from Isaac, Alexander proposed marriage, and Susan accepted. The joining of two prominent families in Susanville was announced; Isaac Roop and the Arnold family endorsed the couple's engagement.

The Roops, The Arnolds & A Girl Named Susan

10

Changes

The Loss of a Patriot

1864

As many travelers passed through Susanville, there was not a day that went by that men, animals, and wagons did not obstruct Main Street. Mishaps occurred every so often, as happened early in 1864 when a man was thrown from his wagon when his team was frightened and ran off. His broken collarbone was cared for with the help from Susanville's citizens, who also rounded up his animals.

Main Street Susanville 1864
Courtesy of Lassen County Historical Society

In the East, 1864

John Roop re-enlisted and re-mustered on January 5, 1864 at the age of twenty. The Seventh Iowa Volunteer Infantry departed Pulaski, Tennessee, for Iowa as they began their thirty-day furlough. The jubilant families welcomed home their soldiers, and John was excited to spend a month at his uncle John's (Isaac's younger brother was also named John Roop) farm in Jackson County, Iowa.

While John had been away at war, his elderly grandparents, Joseph and Susannah Roop, had returned to Seneca County, Ohio, to live with their son David.

The need for more troops increased as the war continued, and the death toll escalated. Two hundred new Union recruits were enlisted, and ordered to prepare for departure from Keokuk Landing, Iowa. On January 27, 1864, John's leave came to an end.

He and the other furloughed men guided the new troops onto a paddle wheeler that steamed south on the Mississippi.

After the men arrived in Cairo, Illinois, at the junction of the Mississippi and Ohio Rivers, they caught transports to Nashville. Following their arrival, the Iowa volunteers boarded railcars for Pulaski. Once in Pulaski, the soldiers then proceeded to Prospect, Tennessee. There they remained on duty at Elk River until John's regiment joined the Atlanta Campaign on May 1, 1864.

Isaiah Roop

On February 24, 1864, Susan's youngest brother, Isaiah, died of smallpox at the age of eighteen. The young patriot, who had entered the army at the age of fifteen, passed away in a hospital at Ironton, Ohio. After losing his arm at Antietam, Isaiah was first transferred to Company Third, Second Battalion, Invalid Corps at Columbus, Ohio. His last assignment was at the Provost Marshall's office in Trenton, Ohio. News of his death did not reach his father, Isaac for three months.

According to a report in the *Sacramento Daily Union* on June 1, 1864, Governor Roop had received the terrible news in May via Atlantic Mail post.

Susan and Alexander postponed their marriage, as a respectable period of mourning was expected. Susan adhered to the rituals of bereavement, and did not attend parties or gatherings during that time.

Isaac's position as postmaster required his immediate return to work, and he insisted that Susan and Alexander should plan to marry before the end of the year.

Isaac was grateful for the love and attention Susan heaped upon him. As shock and despair subsided, both father and daughter prayed for John's wellbeing. Isaac sent a letter to his remaining son, informing him of the death of his brother, as he was not certain if John had received a Union dispatch with the news.

John Roop

By the time John received word of Isaiah's passing, he had just arrived at the Chattahoochee River on a blazing hot summer day. John had little time to grieve, as Union troops held the Chattahoochee River line and spread out in open land as they prepared for the Atlanta Campaign. John and the men of the Iowa Infantry were assigned to the 1st Brigade, 2nd Division, 16th Army Corps. They moved out on July 22, headed for Atlanta where the soldiers would endure five months of battles and skirmishes.

John had penned a reply to his father before he departed for Atlanta. He was excited to share the news of his intention to marry. When John's letter arrived in Susanville it was notated "Soldiers Mail," and Isaac gladly paid the postage upon receipt. In his letter, John explained to both his father and his sister, that while he had been home in Iowa on furlough in January he had become reacquainted with a lovely young lady. John explained that he had met Elenora

SUSANVILLE

Halferty before the war, and had corresponded with her often over the past three years.

The young couple had attended a gathering in John's honor at his uncle's country estate. Elenora came from a large family, and was a cousin to Delilah Brolliar Roop, the wife of John's uncle John (Isaac's younger brother).

Young John wrote in his letter that when the awful war was over, he planned to wed Elenora.

A New County

California

The Surveyor General of California and the Commissioner of the Nevada Territory authorized a boundary survey, which was completed in the fall of 1863. The boundary line was set east of Honey Lake, which placed Susanville and Roop County within the borders of California.* Residents of the Honey Lake Valley conceded that they would remain under Plumas County's jurisdiction until the California Legislature granted them a county of their own.

On April 1, 1864 the Governor of California approved a bill that established the county of Lassen. The boundary line dispute was settled when Roop County in Nevada Territory was declared part of California and a new county was formed. Named after Peter Lassen, an early settler and explorer in northeastern California, the county was formed out of parts of eastern Shasta and eastern Plumas counties.

* Longitude 120 degrees west.

On May 2, Lassen County held its first general election. The voters selected Susanville over Janesville as the new county seat. After the election, county officers were sworn in, and Isaac Roop gifted a block of land to the county for construction of the first jail and courthouse.

In 1864, Susanville's business district was full of activity. The Steward House Hotel was built on the corner of Main and Gay streets. It was a fine large establishment, the first two-story framed building of its size built in town. On the other side of Main Street another blacksmith shop was opened near the tin shop, livery stables, and feed store.

Steward House Main Street Susanville, California
Courtesy of Lassen County Historical Society

SUSANVILLE

Isaac Roop, who reported two thousand five hundred letters had passed through his office between August and October of 1864, efficiently ran the busy Post Office. No less than three hundred newspapers and periodicals were ordered and distributed to Susanville's citizens during the same few months.

Isaac, a thirteen-year member of the Fraternal Order of the Masons, donated the building for the Masonic Hall, which was completed in October.

Lassen Lodge #149 of Susanville hosted a grand all night ball on the occasion of the dedication of their new hall. Friends of the order were invited, as well as the families of lodge members. Alexander Arnold escorted the lovely Miss Susan Roop to the social event.

Main Street Susanville, Looking East - Postcard
Courtesy of ZellamaeArnold Miles

The Roops, The Arnolds & A Girl Named Susan

SUSANVILLE

Part II

The Roops, The Arnolds & A Girl Named Susan

11

The Arnolds

Central Ohio

Alexander Thrall Arnold was born to Nathan and Elizabeth Cutler Arnold on June 12, 1833 in Delaware County, Ohio. He was raised with two older brothers: Cutler Arnold born in 1818, and Leroy Nathan Arnold born in 1824. It was at Nathan Arnold's farm in Delaware County where the Ohio Militia assembled for enlistment, drill, and training.

Alexander's mother Elizabeth died when he was four years old. His father married a second time to Mary Jane Riley, and Alexander's younger half-sister, Mary E. Arnold, was born in 1841.

The Arnold's moved to Morrow County where they were early settlers in Peru Township. Nathan built a cabin in the Allegheny foothills. As more families moved in, the little settlement was referred to as "Denmark."

The 1850 U. S. Federal Census Peru, Morrow, Ohio statics showed:

> Nathan Arnold, farmer, age 53, born Vermont; Jane Arnold, age 40, born Pennsylvania; Mary Arnold, age 9, born Ohio.

At the age of fifteen, Alexander Arnold remained behind in Delaware County after his father moved the family twenty-five miles away to Morrow County. Alexander apprenticed as a tinsmith for two years in Galena. In 1850, after two years of training, he set out alone. Seeking to improve his work prospects, seventeen-year-old Alexander headed south to Franklin County, Ohio.

The Rush to California

Cutler Arnold

Alexander's oldest brother, Cutler, fifteen years his senior, was also eager to join the rush to California. He left his family, including his wife and children, in Ohio and traveled across the plains to Marysville, California. Cutler established himself as a storekeeper, and also did a bit of prospecting during his first year. Impatient to earn enough money to send for his family, Cutler took on extra work. He led pack trains between Rabbit Creek (now La Porte) and Slaughter's Bar (now Goodyear's Bar).

SUSANVILLE

Two years later he sent for his wife, Emily and his four boys: Henry, Leroy, Matthew, and Eugene.

Emily Arnold and the boys left Illinois and departed from New York in July of 1852. The group secured passage on the steamer *Prometheus*. The ship put out from Pier 2, North River, entered New York Bay, and passed out into the Atlantic Ocean as they headed for Nicaragua. Mrs. Arnold and the children crossed Nicaragua safely and arrived in San Francisco on the elegant ship *Pacific*, August 2, 1852. The ship reached the busy California port eleven and a half days after leaving San Juan, with a brief stopover at Acapulco for supplies.

The family was reunited at Marysville, but they did not remain there long, as Cutler was eager to move when new business opportunities became available.

They settled next in Contra Costa County, where the Arnolds engaged in farming land located eight miles east of Martinez. Cutler moved the family five times between 1852 and 1857.

Emily had her fifth son, Edward, in 1854. He was the first of the Arnold's children to be born in California. Shortly thereafter, the family moved to Sacramento where Cutler was proprietor of the Old Eagle Hotel.

When news arrived that Rabbit Creek was in need of a hotel manager, Cutler packed up the family and moved again. Emily, Cutler, and the five boys traveled by pack train out of Marysville to Rabbit Creek where Cutler ran the hotel and store. In 1857, Cutler and his family moved to Rooptown.

Leroy Arnold

Leroy Arnold, Alexander's older brother by nine years, was a veteran of the Mexican-American War. He enlisted on August 15, 1847 in Ottawa, Illinois, and served as a private in the First Illinois Infantry. Leroy was discharged on October 17, 1848 when his term ended, and he journeyed west, joining the Gold Rush. When he arrived in California, Leroy established himself as a merchant in Marysville.

Alexander Arnold

At the age of twenty, Alexander (also referred to as A.T. by family and friends) decided to join his brothers, Cutler and Leroy, in California. As the year 1853 came to a close, A.T. traveled to New York, where he boarded the *North Star* after purchasing a ticket for passage through Panama. Alexander arrived in San Francisco on the *Yankee Blade*, and then journeyed to Martinez to join Cutler on his farm.

Several months after Alexander had settled in California, he received word that he was to become a father. His son, Leroy Dell Arnold, was born on August 17, 1854 in Ohio. The child remained in the East and was raised by his mother, Katherine.*

---

* A.T. may or may not have been married to Katherine, but she did use his last name. He claimed he was widowed on his marriage certificate to Susan, although no proof was found of marriage or divorce, or of him being widowed.

SUSANVILLE

Small Settlements, Big Dreams

Alexander Arnold

Alexander spent the remainder of 1854 working with Cutler in Contra Costa County. In 1855, A.T. left Martinez and headed north to join his brother, Leroy, in Marysville. There was a demand for mule packers to transport goods to the isolated gold rush towns of northeastern California. The steady work and income appealed to Alexander, who signed on as a teamster and liveryman.

It was not long before A.T. relocated to Rabbit Creek in the mountains of northwest Sierra County, where he joined Cutler, then the proprietor of the local hotel. The settlement was the center of navigation in the movement of supplies to all the mines within thirty miles of town. Situated in the rugged Northern Sierra, Rabbit Creek was crowded with the constant loading of wagons and unloading of teams.

The mules were heavily loaded with building and mining supplies, as well as food and mail, as Alexander led the pack train to each settlement. He traveled up and down the steep ravines and canyon trails between each isolated mining camp. The miners who worked the river bars and placer diggings were excited when the packer arrived. Mail from home was valued more than food or supplies.

As more miners and emigrants arrived, new roads were surveyed and built. The freight wagon soon replaced pack trains in the transportation of heavy loads. Freight companies contracted with teamsters to haul their loads. The company boss determined which goods were going out and the destination. The teamsters loaded the wagons and chose the best hitch to be used—multiple pairs of mules, horses, or oxen—to transport the loads. Along the roads to remote camps way stations were built where teamsters and their animals stopped to rest.

The strongest pair of animals were harnessed at the back of the team, directly in the front of the wagon. They were called the wheelers. If mules or horses were used, the teamster rode on the left rear wheeler and controlled the team using reins attached to each pair of animals. He also used a jerk line to communicate with the lead animal. With oxen, the bullwhacker walked alongside the left rear wheeler and cracked a long bullwhip to control his stock.

The teamsters had to be strong and skillful in order to manage the huge freight wagons and to control the team on rough, steep and winding roads. The heavy wagons advanced slowly, with the men walking much of the time while they kept a close eye on the animals and each loaded wagon. If the animals trudged through rain swollen creeks and mud, so did the teamsters.

1857

Cutler Arnold

In 1857 Cutler left his family in the care of his brother, Alexander, in Rabbit Creek, while he moved to Rooptown. He planned to build the first hostelry in the small settlement. Cutler began construction of the log hotel in the spring of that year.

Cutler's oldest son, Henry Arnold, signed the Roop House Register on April 3, 1857. He recorded that he had arrived via Rabbit Creek. Henry and Cutler's neighbors helped to finish the small building on June 9.

They spent the evening in friendly drink and celebration. Cutler then went back over the mountains to fetch his wife Emily and their children.

A.T. was enlisted to assist Cutler in transporting his large family back over the Sierra Nevada. It was a tiring journey as the group traveled by horseback along narrow mountain trails. Alexander used his keen knowledge of the remote trails and his skill with the animals to guide the family safely into Rooptown.

The Roop House Register of June 25, 1857 recorded: "Cut Arnold and family arrived today all well." Cutler and Emily's first daughter, Emma Eunice Arnold, was born in 1857.

The Roop House Register recorded the numbers passing through the valley between August 2, 1857 and October 4, 1857:

> 99 trains or parties
> 306 wagons and carriages
> 665 horses and mules
> 16,937 cattle
> 835 men
> 254 women
> 390 children

Leroy Arnold

In 1857, Leroy also decided to join his brother in Rooptown. Leroy had traveled through the Honey Lake Valley briefly in 1856 while on a prospecting expedition, and because he enjoyed the area, Leroy decided to relocate. He assisted Cutler in building the log hotel, and he stayed on to assist with the establishment of the business and the stocking of merchandise for sale.

After the hostelry opened for business, Leroy headed out to do a bit of mining. He spent many years exploring the rivers and canyons of Northern California as well as the mineral ledges located in the Black Rock and Humboldt regions east of Honey Lake Valley.

1858

Alexander (A. T.) Arnold

Alexander was a seasoned teamster who passed over the mountain roads between Rabbit Creek (named La Porte in 1857) and the Honey Lake Valley. When his loads were delivered and he had a few leisure hours to himself, A.T. panned the streams in search of gold.

Alexander left home at the age of fifteen, and had spent ten years on his own. He was ready to put

SUSANVILLE

down roots, so he joined his brothers in Rooptown, which was named Susanville by the time he arrived in 1858.

The fast growing frontier town lured many a settler in 1858, and by fall of the year A.T. had joined his family at Cutler's Hotel. After establishing a permanent home, Alexander easily found work hauling freight out of Susanville.

As the movement of freight by wagon increased in Northern California, pack trains were consigned to the narrowest and steepest roads in the most remote canyon settlements. As emigrants continued to move into the Honey Lake Valley, the need for supplies increased. Horse, oxen, and mule teams were used to pull wagons loaded with freight. The animals that were used depended upon the destination and the load. The wagons were able to move more than the pack trains could handle.

Alexander signed on as a freighter. He departed Susanville over some of the same roads that the passenger and mail stages traveled over. His heavy wagon twisted and pounded over the dirt roads between settlements, where he stopped just long enough to drop off his load.

In 1858 transcontinental mail service began via overland stagecoach to Susanville. Although much of the Atlantic mail continued to be delivered by steam ship to San Francisco, the new overland mail delivery system increased communication between the East and West. The mail was transported by stage from St. Louis, to Salt Lake City, and then on to California and Oregon via Nobles Pass.

Weekly mail service to the Honey Lake Valley and Susanville was consigned by way of established routes:

- Marysville Route – from La Porte via Quincy, including the American Valley and Indian Valley, to Susanville
- Oroville Route – Bidwell's Bar to Susanville
- Shasta Route – Shasta City via Noble's Pass to Susanville
- Genoa to Carson Valley via Eagle Pass through Washoe, Truckee, and Long Valley to Susanville
- Carson Valley via the Humboldt River to the junction at Nobles Pass

1859

During the summer of 1859, emigration through Honey Lake Valley peaked. Animals were dying on the trail between the Humboldt Sink and Carson Valley. Many emigrants chose the Nobles Trail where grass and water was sufficient. Three thousand head of cattle were driven from Missouri through the Honey Lake Valley by one outfit, alone. Twelve hundred wagons and four thousand people had passed through Susanville by the first day of September, 1859. At summer's end, there were two hundred head of horses in the valley, corralled and

SUSANVILLE

Mountain Camp, Sierra Nevada
Daniel Jenks described the scene he drew that day in 1859:
"Drawing on paper shows a camp in the heart of a forest of tall pines. Covered wagons rest, their wheels nearly hidden by tall grass in the clearing. Men and women cook over a large open fire near a stream in the Sierra Nevada Mountains, having left Susanville, California that morning, on Saturday August 13, 1859, and made camp here." Daniel A. Jenks, 1827-1869.
Courtesy of the Library of Congress

ready for transfer to the California Stage Company. The final additions to the herd were ten horses, all bred from splendid stock that had been driven across the plains from Illinois.

A few of the emigrants chose to remain in Susanville and establish businesses that helped to advance the development of the frontier town. Forty marriageable ladies had settled in the upper end of the valley during that season, a notable statistic, as men far outnumbered women in the early settlement years.

There was a baby boom in the summer of 1859, when five babies were born in Susanville during the month of June. Cutler Arnold's wife, Emily, gave birth to their seventh child, a healthy boy named George.

Alexander's brother, Leroy, was a bachelor until the age of thirty-five. In the summer of 1859, Leroy met a lovely young lady named Mariah Harpham. They were married in Susanville on November 17, 1859, three weeks before Mariah turned eighteen. During the cool clear days of late autumn, the Arnold family hosted a small wedding celebration.

On Christmas Eve, Susanville was covered in a blanket of white snow eighteen inches deep that had fallen during the week.

Provisions were plentiful in the Honey Lake Valley, but the residents of Carson Valley sent word that they were in need of flour and feed for their livestock. Six wagon teams from Susanville answered the call and delivered the needed provisions. The convoy returned to Susanville, just in time for holiday festivities.

SUSANVILLE

12

Many Roads Traveled

The Honey Lake Wagon Road

1860

During the summer of 1860, Colonel F. W.
Lander led a government expedition to complete a
survey and essential improvements on the primary
emigrant wagon road west of Fort Kearney. The route
from Fort Kearney ran through South Pass in the
Rocky Mountains, and then along the Nobles Trail in
the Sierra Nevada.

After Lander's crew completed their work,
which included sinking wells and digging reservoirs,
the Nobles Emigrant Trail was thereafter referred to
as the Honey Lake Wagon Road. Susanville quickly
increased in importance and recognition throughout
the territory.

The statistics in the 1860 U.S. Federal Census Honey Lake Valley, Plumas County, California showed these details:

> Cutler Arnold, farmer, age 41; Emily Arnold, age 41; Henry Arnold, age 21; Leroy Arnold, age 18; Mathew Arnold, age 16; Eugene Arnold, age 14; Edward Arnold, age 6; Eunice Arnold, age 3; George Arnold, age 1.

> Cutler Arnold, value of real estate, $3000, value of personal estate, $1200
> Leroy Arnold, merchant, age 32
> Leroy Arnold, value of personal estate, $250.

Leroy's wife Mariah was not listed in the census. Alexander Arnold was not listed in the census enumerated on July 23, 1860, as he was away freighting.

In Iowa, the 1860 U.S. Federal Census Tipton, Cedar County Iowa shows Alexander's son living with this mother:

> Kate E. Arnold, dressmaker, age 29, born Ohio; Leroy D. Arnold, age 6, born Ohio, living with the Daniels family.

Alexander was frequently gone for weeks at a time. During the peak of hauling season, he could be away from home for several months, as he was in the summer of 1860. He traveled along the busy freight roads of northeastern California and Nevada Territory, transporting merchandise in and out of Susanville. On a midsummers day in 1860, A.T. loaded a wagon and departed from Virginia City. Bound for Red Bluff, he set out from the Comstock and followed the freight road through the Truckee Meadows, then into the Honey Lake Valley.

When Alexander arrived in Susanville from Virginia City, he checked in at the freight office on Main Street and the team was changed out. Freight officials inspected the shipment and recorded the delivery in the company ledger. Teamsters offloaded the freight consigned for Susanville, and then loaded the wagons with additional supplies destined for Red Bluff.

It was important that teamsters checked that the load was evenly distributed in the wagon, the harnesses were secure, and the animals were fit. When fully loaded, the freight wagons were slow and heavy, they could sink to the axles in muddy terrain and more than one teamster was needed to handle them. Often many loaded wagons followed each other into towns, whose streets became blocked by their hefty loads.

A.T. stopped to check in with his family and enjoyed a home cooked meal. Alexander was not surprised to learn that his brother, Leroy, was off prospecting and had deposited his pregnant wife, Mariah, with Cutler and Emily.

Freighting on Main Street Susanville California
Courtesy of Lassen County Historical Society

With a fresh pack of food that Emily had prepared for him, Alexander prepared to leave town. When the load was secured and the animals harnessed, A.T. double checked the hitch and ascended the mountains.

As Alexander tracked along the Honey Lake and Marysville wagon road, he enjoyed the sight of lush meadows and meandering streams where valley livestock grazed and fattened in the summer sun. Pine and fir trees provided welcome shade along the passage, although the dust from the road permeated everything that was not covered.

Alexander descended into Marysville, an agricultural town ideally situated on the banks above the Yuba and Feather rivers. Accessible by

SUSANVILLE

stage or steamer from Sacramento, Marysville was a hub of activity. Much of the trade goods destined for the northern mines and small settlements passed through Marysville.

After he departed from Marysville, A.T. began the ninety-mile trip north to Red Bluff (also referred to as Red Bluffs). He crossed the Sacramento River at Tehama and arrived after the final fourteen-mile pull.

The steamer *Queen City* had just put in at the steamboat landing after a short stopover in Colusa. There were one hundred United States Army Troops on board the *Queen City* when Alexander reached the hot and busy town.

The soldiers had departed from Benicia Barracks and were assigned for duty at Fort Crook in eastern Shasta County. The men were required to report to the fort commander upon arrival and then were sent out to patrol the northern California emigrant roads. Their primary duty was to safeguard the movement of freight, settlers, and travelers along the isolated wagon roads.

Alexander stopped at a roadhouse in Red Bluff and secured an area for his team. The mules, horses, and oxen that hauled goods over the busy freight roads needed to be watered, fed, and rested daily.

A.T. shared a noisy meal at a table with other teamsters, who all seemed to talk at once, sharing news and travel stories. Many of the same teamsters met up time and again on their routine trips in and out of supply towns such as Red Bluff. Alexander was glad to learn that funds had recently been secured to complete the emigrant road from Red Bluff to the Honey Lake Valley.

The Red Bluff road was scheduled to open in time for the seasonal arrival of emigrants from the East. The new road tracked to the east out of Red Bluff, a route that provided abundant feed and water for the animals. As the road ascended in altitude, it meandered east past Antelope Mills, Mill Creek, and Deer Creek Meadows, where the road then reached the west branch of the Feather River. At a crossroads seven miles east of Lassen Meadows, the road joined the Honey Lake and Marysville wagon road, twenty-five miles distant from the Honey Lake Valley.

The Humboldt

1861

Located one hundred thirty miles east of the Honey Lake Valley, the Humboldt Mining District was rich in gold and silver-bearing quartz. It ran the entire length of the mountain range that paralleled the Humboldt River. The Humboldt mines were located south of the emigrant road at Lassen Meadows, the same road that had been cleared by Lander's expedition the previous year. More than five hundred men were reported to be prospecting in the Humboldt region in the summer of 1861.

Cutler left his brother, Leroy, behind at the Humboldt to try his hand at mining there, and returned home to Susanville after completing a freight run along the Honey Lake Wagon Road.

Overland emigrants continued to journey West during the Civil War, many by means of the Honey

SUSANVILLE

Lake Wagon road. The route was the preferred choice for travelers seeking land and opportunity in the small agricultural communities north of Sacramento. After the emigrants passed the Humboldt River at Rabbit Hole Springs on their westward journey, they arrived at the junction of the Applegate and Honey Lake Wagon roads.

Emigrants who had previously taken the Applegate Trail reported that the dry and rocky terrain was too hard on the animals. Many travelers opted for the Honey Lake Wagon Road (Nobles Trail) to Susanville. After arriving in Susanville they were able to purchase provisions at a reasonable cost and have their animals re-shod when necessary.

Alexander Arnold noticed an increase in the number of emigrants taking up land and settling in Northern California. On the first Saturday in September of 1861, A.T. had just passed Lassen Meadows with a load of merchandise when he encountered between two hundred and three hundred immigrant wagons bound for Tehama and Yuba counties.

When A.T. returned to Susanville after a long season freighting, he discovered that a great number of men from Honey Lake, including his brother Leroy, had departed for the Humboldt mines. They were caught up in the excitement of the new strikes that were reported daily.

On August 30, 1861, ex-Governor Roop accompanied wagons loaded with twelve tons of ore taken from a claim on the east bank of the Humboldt River. The ore was packed in wooden boxes and transported from the Humboldt mines to Red Bluff, at a cost of one hundred sixty dollars per ton. Eight tons of silver ore was loaded on the steamer *Swan* at Red Bluff, and forwarded to San Francisco for assay.

As 1861 came to a close, the Arnold family was healthy, prosperous, and growing. Leroy and Mariah had welcomed their first child, Katherine Arnold during the year. The Arnold's hotel had been sold two years before, which provided the family with a sizable reserve. By 1863 the Arnold's had a store located near the barbershop on the southwest corner of Main and Gay Streets.

Lured by the steady income and his eagerness to travel, Cutler returned to the wagon roads hauling freight. He and Emily had seven children—six boys and a girl. Their youngest child, George, was two years old, and their oldest, Henry, was twenty-two.

Alexander's son, Leroy Dell Arnold, was seven years old and lived with his mother in Iowa. A.T. was eager to bring the boy out West, but did not have proper accommodations for a young lad.

Freight Haulers

1862-1864

In 1862 the younger Arnold children attended school, and Cutler and Emily's older boys were busy supplementing the family income with new ventures of their own.

Henry had just turned twenty-three, and he managed horses and cattle at a camp between Willow

SUSANVILLE

Creek and Soldier Bridge. His younger brothers, Leroy age twenty, and Matthew age eighteen, occasionally helped Henry with the livestock.

The boys could also be found riding along with Cutler or A.T., hauling freight on the roads of northern California and the Humboldt region. Teamster's wages varied between forty and eighty dollars per month, depending upon the hardship of the route, the size of the team and the proportions of the load.

As covered in chapter nine, Susan Roop had settled in her new home in Susanville at the beginning of 1863. As the pleasant days of spring turned into the hot days of summer, the wagons and stock that traveled past the Roop's home on Main Street increased daily. Over two hundred eighty teams passed through Susanville between June 1 and July 15 of 1863 on the way to the Humboldt region alone. The summertime weather was favorable, which augmented the growth and production of crops that thrived in the valley during the season.

Alexander Arnold made Susan's acquaintance shortly after her arrival in Susanville, during the time he assisted with the construction of the new Masonic hall and they became friends.

Alexander joined Lassen Lodge #149 as the new Masonic hall was being built. When he was not out of town freighting, A.T. was active in town affairs. He supported the growth of Susanville businesses, and worked to secure the safety of travelers.

It was a hectic year for those who journeyed on the road to and from the Humboldt. Soldiers patrolled the main wagon roads, and local citizens banded together to protect home and property. Fear of hostile attacks on parties traveling the roads of northeastern

California forced Alexander and Henry Arnold to answer an alarm that came in from landowners in Surprise Valley.

In late August of 1863, a dozen armed men were mounted and headed out to patrol and protect pioneers, ranches, and livestock in the remote vast valley south of Fort Bidwell. Soldiers from Smoke Creek barracks joined the patrol.

The group spotted Paiute Indians who fled into Nevada, and they scared off Modoc Indians who crossed over the Oregon border. Although the men saw signal fires and Indians on the hills above the valley, no skirmish took place. The patrol group came upon the men who were surveying California's eastern boundary line. Under the night skies of August, the men enjoyed a campfire together in the isolation of the high desert country.

Adventurers traveled the wagon roads to the Humboldt and then north to the Boise region when gold was discovered there in 1862. By 1863 the trek of miners and freight teams traveling through the Honey Lake Valley had increased. The roads were clogged with wagons transporting lumber and provisions to the Boise River region. The shortest and easiest route was to follow the stream of miners who trekked through the Great Basin, out to the Humboldt mines, and then north into Idaho Territory. There was plenty of water, grass, and wood along the route.

As spring rains subsided in early May of 1864, Cutler Arnold and his fourth son, Eugene, then sixteen, began their first of four years freighting together in Nevada and in southwestern Idaho Territory. After

SUSANVILLE

confirming that Emily and the younger children were well set, Cutler and Eugene set out through the Jordan Valley to Silver City.

Eugene enjoyed the time he spent on the road and learned valuable skills from his father. He would grow to be a keen stock handler and had a sharp mind for business. The loads they transported included a variety of merchandise that was needed in the boomtowns of the West: building materials, mining supplies, and food staples, such as potatoes, bacon, and flour.

Alexander hauled freight loads between Red Bluff and Susanville, a good one hundred and ten miles one way. The road paralleled the north fork of the Feather River. Alexander wished to remain close Susanville, as he had recently become engaged to Susan Roop.

During the hot summer months, A.T. enjoyed traveling on the wagon roads that took him through the steep canyons of the Sierra Nevada. There he found clear running creeks and green meadows at nearly every stop. He had driven the same Sierra roads for the previous eight years, and he knew them well. He had no desire, as his brother Cutler did, to trek into the heat of the high desert region through the Humboldt and then north to the Idaho mines.

As the Civil War raged on, soldiers in California were reassigned to battlefields in the East. When they departed, a volunteer militia was enlisted to assume responsibility of protecting the West.

In the Honey Lake Valley, a company was

organized in July and mustered into service on September 28, 1864. Referred to as the Honey Lake Rangers, the 5th Brigade was an unattached Cavalry Company. Their members numbered over fifty men and included Isaac Roop and Alexander Arnold, as well as Cutler's sons, Henry, Leroy, and Matthew Arnold. Henry, an experienced scout, had by that time spent numerous years patrolling the wagon roads of Northeastern California in the company of state troops.

The Susanville Masonic Lodge hosted a grand ball in October to celebrate the completion of their new hall. Fraternity members and their families danced the night away, many staying until the first light of dawn. Alexander Arnold and his betrothed, Susan Roop, spent a nice evening in the company of her father.

SUSANVILLE

13

Marriage and Children

Mr. & Mrs. Arnold

1864-1865

Isaac Roop and Nancy Gardner had been married on December 24, 1840. Twenty-four years later, almost to the day, their daughter, Susan, married Alexander Arnold on December 27, 1864. The marriage of Alexander Arnold and Susan Roop was entered in the Lassen County Recorder's ledger[*]:

---

[*] This text presented on the next page is exactly as entered in the Lassen County Recorder's Ledger.

State of California
County of Lassen

To any Judge Justice of the Peace
Preacher or Minister of the Gospel
Greetings you are hereby authorized to unite in
Wedlock the bonds of Matrimony Mr. A. T. Arnold
and Miss Susan Roop and of this license and your
certificate make use return to this office within thirty
days from the date of such certificate. Given under my
hand with the seal of our county court affixed this 27th
day of Dec 1864   A. A. Smith Co. Clerk

Certificate of Marriage
Susanville Dec. 27th 1864
This certifies that I I. J. Harvey a County Judge
in and for the County of Lassen
united in Marriage in Susanville County of Lassen
on the 27th day of December
One Thousand eight hundred and sixty four

A.T. Arnold	and	Susan Roop
Residence Susanville		Residence Susanville
Lassen County		Lassen County
Age Thirty one		Age Twenty three
Color White		Color White
Place of Nativity - Ohio		Place of Nativity - Ohio
Single or Widowed-Widowed		Single or Widowed–Single

In accordance with laws of the State of California
I. J. Harvey County Judge
Filed Dec. 28th 1864
A. A. Smith Recorder
By H. L. Spargur Deputy
Certificate of Marriage

SUSANVILLE

It was a cold windy day as the newlyweds settled comfortably into the Roop residence on Main Street with Isaac. Their marriage was publicized in the *Sacramento Daily Union* on February 7, 1865.

The End of The Civil War

John Roop

Following the capture of Atlanta, John Roop and the Seventh Iowa were assigned to the 1st Brigade, 4th Division, 15th Army Corps. The men pursued the Confederates into Alabama during the month of October 1864, and then began the March to the Sea on November 15. Although John was wounded during the campaign, he was deemed fit enough to continue the advance across Georgia. The Army of the Tennessee, led by General William T. Sherman, ended its successful six-week march when it secured the seaport at Savannah on December 21, 1864.

John Roop and the soldiers of the Army of the Tennessee marched north into South Carolina early in February of 1865. After securing Columbia, Sherman's troops moved into North Carolina during the final few months of the Civil War.

The Campaign of the Carolinas ended with the occupation of Raleigh on April 14, and the surrender of the Confederate Army on April 18, 1865. John marched through Richmond, Virginia, and then on to Washington, D.C. for the Grand Review on May 24.

After arriving in Louisville, Kentucky, in

the heat of midsummer, Private John Roop and his companions mustered out of service on July 12, 1865. The triumphant men of the Seventh Iowa Infantry returned home to Keokuk County, amid cheers and celebration.

Wedding arrangements had been made prior to John's arrival, and after spending four years away at war he was only too happy to immediately meet his bride at the altar. John Roop, age 21, and Elenora Halferty, age 20, were married on August 21, 1865. In attendance to celebrate the wedding were Elenora's family and John's uncle John and his wife Delilah, along with their children, Susan, Joseph W., Mary, Martha, and Arthur Roop.

During the years John was away fighting for the Union, his elderly grandparents, Joseph and Susannah Roop, had left Iowa and moved to Seneca County, Ohio. Their son David, who also cared for their younger daughter, Elizabeth, had looked after them. However, both of his grandparents, and his aunt had died by the time John returned home from the war.

Susannah Roop, age 70, died June 19, 1864. Their daughter, Elizabeth Roop, age 32, died May 2, 1865. Two weeks later Joseph Roop, age 72, died on May 16, 1865. All were buried in the Dunkard Cemetery in Bloomfield Ohio.

John was sad to learn of his grandparents' passing. He became very close to them, after having lived with them for many years after his father Isaac moved west.

SUSANVILLE

The Arnolds

The Fourth of July celebration of 1865 brought out Susanville's citizens to watch the Honey Lake Rangers parade in full dress on Main Street. Susan and Isaac praised Alexander, who cut a fine figure in his uniform. People spent the day enjoying food and refreshment before the merriment ended with a dance.

Isaac completed his first year as District Attorney of Lassen County on September 6, 1865. The jail was being constructed on a block of land that he had gifted to the county the previous year, and it was scheduled for completion late in the year.

On a pleasant fall day, Susan announced that she was expecting a child in June, much to the delight of her husband and her father.

During the year of 1865, Alexander noticed many settlers taking up land and building homes along the wagon roads he traveled. During fair weather, he freighted over familiar northeastern California roads, returning home as often as possible.

Alexander's brother, Cutler, and his nephew, Eugene, followed the busy wagon roads to the Ruby City and Silver City mines. The northern roads were full of activity with teamsters, wagons, livestock, and excited prospectors, who hired pack trains to transport them to the Idaho region.

Alexander had plenty of work freighting in and out of Susanville. His trip in the fall was typical of the many loads he hauled along the same roads he had traveled for many years. Immigrants were moving into the tiny hamlets of the Sierra where some settlements boasted large-scale mining operations.

He traveled along the Tehama County Wagon Road (toll road) late in November of 1865, and stopped to rest his team at Big Meadows, thirty miles from Susanville. He then headed his wagon southeast to Greenville, where Blood's Mill was crushing gold quartz, and another mill was under construction. Five miles farther up the road, in the southwest corner of the valley, Alexander arrived at the Crescent Mine. One hundred and fifty men were employed there to operate the two stamp mills and hoisting works.

After two days on the road from Red Bluff via Big Meadows, Alexander arrived at Indian Valley. The fertile grain-growing area was surrounded by mountains, rich in the precious metals of gold and copper. Taylorsville was located on the south side of the valley and boasted three hotels, two livery stables, two blacksmith shops, as well as several stores.

After his load was delivered Alexander hastily returned to Susanville and a home cooked meal.

1866-1868

During the winter months, Alexander worked in the livery, tending horses, and repairing farm and freight wagons.

His brother, Leroy continued to mine at Black Rock in the Humboldt region. Leroy's prolonged absence was too difficult for his young wife Mariah. She became acquainted with another man, and

SUSANVILLE

married Abraham Bower in January of 1866.* The new couple took the children—Katherine Arnold, age five, and Frank Arnold, age three—to Siskiyou County. Leroy consoled himself with work at the mines.

The Bowers lived in Scott Valley and had the first of five children of their own late the same year. They raised all the children, including Katherine and Frank Arnold, and grew old together in the scenic valley surrounded by mountains and streams near Fort Jones, California.

---

* As was so often the case in these early days, there is no proof of a legal divorce between Leroy and Mariah.

The Old Livery Stable North End of Main Street,
Susanville, Looking East
Courtesy of Lassen County Historical Society

Family Life in a Thriving Little Town

On June 21, 1866 a daughter was born to Mr. and Mrs. A.T. Arnold. Named after her mother, Susan M. Arnold, was lovingly nicknamed "Susey" by her grandfather.

While Susan stayed home with her new daughter, Alexander and the local teamsters were off freighting most days of every week. While her husband was away, Susan and her baby were watched over by attentive grandfather, Isaac.

Although his post office and District Attorney duties kept him busy most days, Isaac was home in the evenings to enjoy a supper and the evenings with his daughter and granddaughter.

The U.S. mail and express stage line from Oroville and Chico departed every two days to Ruby City and Silver City, arriving in Idaho within four days during fair weather. After the mail and passenger coach departed the Sacramento Valley, it met up with another stage at Big Meadows that ran out to Indian Valley. The main stage route that left Big Meadows went through Susanville, out to the Black Rock region, then to Fort McGarry (Summit Lake), and on to the Idaho mines.

The stage traveled day and night, stopping only to change horses. Passengers were allowed thirty pounds of baggage at no extra charge. Those travelers who exceeded the limit, paid an additional thirty cents per pound. The fares levied were sixty-two dollars to ride the stage from Oroville through to Silver City, Idaho Territory, or ten dollars for travelers disembarking in Susanville.

SUSANVILLE

Susan had good reason to worry about her husband's safety while he was freighting. Thieves roamed the desolate frontier wagon roads, looking to steal cash, coin, and merchandise. Two teamsters were robbed on June 22, 1866 as they traveled along the Butte road from Susanville. The teamsters were forced to surrender about sixty dollars as their pockets were turned out, and also to relinquish their boots. By the time a stagecoach found them, the robbers had vanished.

On Monday morning, August 28, 1866, the Susanville Chico Stage was robbed after leaving Mountain Meadows. The six passengers on board were relieved of all their cash. The masked robbers collected a total of sixteen hundred dollars. General Bidwell's hired man was the biggest loser of the group, as his pocket was cleared of six hundred dollars.

Although military patrols were stationed along busy stage and wagon roads, it was difficult to cover the wide expanse of territory settled by the pioneers. Fully armed, mounted, and equipped cavalry units were stationed in remote outposts to protect citizens, mail, and trade goods. They were prepared to relieve hardship at a moment's notice and, on occasion, retrieved the company physician to assist a poor soul in distress.

In the summer of 1866, troops were moved to locations where the most activity was reported. General McDowell ordered the men in Company A at Camp Union in Sacramento to move out to Fort Bidwell. A good number of the men from Company B at Fort Churchill were sent to the post at Fort McGarry, northeast of Soldier Meadows, on the road from Susanville.

Susanville was a thriving little town full of enterprising settlers who supplied the many travelers passing through the Honey Lake Valley. On the busiest days during the summer months, as many as fifty teams could be counted passing through Susanville.

The Steward House Hotel, located on the corner of Main and Gay Streets, was a favorite stop for travelers. It offered fine food, barroom drinks, billiards, and overnight accommodations. The stage office was located at the Steward House where freight, mail, and passengers were moved on routes to and from:

> Chico, Susanville, and Idaho
> Susanville and Oroville
> Susanville and Virginia City

Stage Coach
George B. Long stage driver in front of the
Johnston Hotel, Main Street, Susanville
Courtesy of the Lassen County Historical Society

SUSANVILLE

Conveniently located near the stagecoach office were a variety of shops that catered to travelers, including a blacksmith shop, wagon repair, drug store, mercantile, saloon, livery, and feed stable.

In May of 1867 Alexander set off to the Black Rock region where Leroy still worked the ledges. Although the region had disappointed many a miner, Leroy remained for years, even after the rush was over.

Alexander earned a good wage by hauling aggregate. He transported four-horse loads of Black Rock ore to Dall's Mill in Washoe Valley. The route from the mines was full of activity, and as wagons passed along, the road became choked with dust. Alexander enjoyed the landscape as he approached the mill site, which was located in a scenic valley surrounded by the forested Sierra Nevada.

Susan Roop's Family

On June 30, 1867 Susan's grandparents, John and Jane Gardner, sold their property in Wayne County, Ohio, and moved to LaSalle County, Illinois. Their sons, John Jr. and David, moved west with them, transporting their families to a scenic valley along the Illinois River.

The four-hundred-mile journey was difficult for John Gardner, Sr. and he did not survive the year. His widow, Jane, first lived with their son, David, and then moved in with another son, John, in her later years. Both wagon makers, the brothers lived next to each other in the city of Ottawa, Illinois.

Isaac was fond of his late wife's family, and often wrote to John Gardner Jr. They had remained close even after Nancy's death. John and his wife, Lucy, had just welcomed their third child, Burton Gardner, into the world when they received a letter sent from Susanville, California.

The letter from Isaac to his brother-in-law read:[*]

Susanville Ca   April 12, 1868
John Gardner Esq

My dear Bro
        I received your note of Feb 23rd on the 7th and I do assure you that we was much pleased to hear from you again – but we was very sorry to hear that Farthes was no more. I would have been glad to have seen him ere he died. I wish that Mother was out here and live with us. As we have a good home –Susey and her Husband is still liveing with me. So is Ephraim, I am still in the Post Office and the District Attorney Office. We have been very busy this spring in settling out fruit trees. We rais a larg amount of fruit of all kinds and set out this spring over eight thousand grafts. I wish that you and wife and the Babies could call and see us. Suseys Babe is now about twenty two months old. She is a very

---

[*] This letter is presented with spelling and punctuation exactly as Isaac wrote it.

SUSANVILLE

*smart child – I named this River here
and this town after Susey* and I named
her child Susey after the River and
Town – So you see I have lotts of Suseys.
We are well and have been very hearty.*

*Do you think that Mother would
come out if I would send for her. I wish
to God that she was here to spend her
last days with us. I know that she
would live longer here than there, and
I could make it comfortable here for
her. Mother will you come – you and
my Son and his wife could come out
together, please let me hear from you.
I dont hardly think that I will ever get
back home again, it may be when the
Rail Road is completed though I may
take a flying visit back there again.
Money is to scarce I have plenty of
good property but no money it is very
scarce here I run through with about
two thousand dollars the last eighteen
months in the Silver Mines, but I shall
try it again this season make a spoon
or spoil a man. Ephraim starts in about
twenty days on a prospecting ---- north
some two hundred miles. Prospecting
for new Gold Diggins he will be gone
some five or six months, he says that*

* Isaac may have believed he named the river after his daughter,
but William Nobles had already named the river after his wife,
also named Susan. Nobles had passed through the Honey Lake
Valley in 1852 while blazing a new immigrant trail, Isaac arrived
a year later.

this trip will wind up his prospecting, if he don't make a nois this time he will never mine any more – My kindness Love to Mother. May God Bless her and make her last days easy and pleasant, my love to your wife and babies. Dont fail to answer on receipt of this.

Yours Eternally,

(A kiss to mother for me)

Isaac Roop

Susan and A.T. welcomed a son into the family on August 23, 1868. Isaac Newton Arnold was named after his grandfather. Grandfather Isaac was pleased that the Roop's home was full of activity as Susan was busy caring for an infant and her two-year-old daughter. With his family growing, Alexander abandoned freight work out of town and stayed close to home.

The Black Rock mines had been abandoned by early 1868. Deemed worthless, the mines did not produce even a trace of precious metals after tons of ore was milled in January and February of 1868. A few hardy souls remained in the Humboldt region. Alexander's brother, Leroy, prospected in the area for nearly thirty years, sure that in the next ledge he would hit pay dirt.

14

A Sad Farewell

Ventura County

1868

Cutler Arnold and Family

Cutler Arnold left Susanville in 1868 and moved to Santa Barbara County, taking along wife Emily and their children still living at home: Matthew age 24, Eugene age 22, Edward age 14, Emma (Eunice) age 11, George age 9, and Fanny age 4. The family settled in San Buenaventura on a large plot of fertile land.

The Arnolds were pioneer settlers in Hueneme, an area of Ventura County that split from Santa Barbara County soon after their arrival. Matthew and Eugene Arnold each took up their own one hundred and sixty acres of farmland. Matthew bought a ranch in 1868 in Ventura where he lived with his wife, Eliza. Eugene engaged in grain production and raised standard and thoroughbred horses.

The Roops

During the fall of 1868, twenty tons of ripe juicy apples were harvested from Isaac Roop's orchard, which was full to bursting with seven hundred apple trees. The crop was especially large due to the perfect weather conditions during the growing season. Susan spent many a pleasant autumn day baking, and putting up preserves and jam. The harvested apples that did not fit into cold storage were sold, which allowed the family to purchase food staples that would last them through the winter.

The Last Trip

Ephraim Roop

On November 8, 1868, Ephraim Roop left Susanville on a trip to Ohio to visit family members whom he had not seen in sixteen years. His brothers

David, Israel, and Jonas, all lived in Seneca County. His younger siblings, Joseph N. and Mary Jane, lived in Ashland County with their own growing families.

As mentioned previously, Ephraim's younger sister, Elizabeth, and his parents, Joseph and Susannah Roop, had passed away several years before his planned departure. They were all buried in the Dunkard Cemetery in Bloomville, Ohio.

Isaac declined Ephraim's invitation to accompany him on the trip to Ohio. Isaac's work commitments prevented a lengthy absence and, most importantly, he would not leave Susan and the babies that he adored.

Ephraim bid his brother and niece farewell. As he set out from Susanville, he promised to send them a letter. His traveling companions were Lassen County residents E.G. Bangham, Fred Hines, and George Johnston. They all planned to visit their families in the East.

When the group arrived in San Francisco, they booked passage on a steam ship to New York via the Isthmus of Panama. At 11:00 a.m. on Monday morning, November 14, 1868, Ephraim and his companions left San Francisco and put out to sea, sailing south to Panama. They cruised aboard the sidewheel steamer *Golden Age*, owned by the Pacific Mail and Steamship Company.

When the *Golden Age* arrived in Panama Bay, several of the passengers were infected with small pox. A Steamship Company agent removed three of the passengers who were sick with the virus, and delivered them to the infirmary. Two of the men who had departed from Susanville were among those transported to the clinic. One survived the illness and the other did not.

Fred Hines survived and continued his journey to the east after he recovered. But his friend, Ephraim Roop, did not recover. On November 28, 1868, at the age of forty-seven, Ephraim Roop died in the government hospital in Panama, just twenty days after leaving Susanville.

Isaac was shocked and saddened to learn of his brother's death from the same dreadful disease that had taken the life of his dear son, Isaiah. Ephraim and Isaac had been close companions since the day in 1852 when Ephraim arrived in Shasta after traveling the overland emigrant trail. The two brothers were similar in character and were closest in age of all Joseph and Susannah Roop's eleven children. Never married, Ephraim had relished the time he spent with Isaac, Susan, Alexander, and the children.

Isaac sent a letter to Ohio informing family members of Ephraim's death. Ephraim may have been exposed to the disease before he left Susanville, or possibly upon his arrival in San Francisco, as many cities in California had reported smallpox outbreaks in 1868.

The Final Goodbye

1869

Grieving the loss of his brother, Isaac took ill two months later during the coldest days of winter in 1869. Not one to rest when ailing, Isaac continued working until he was exhausted and bedridden with pneumonia. Although Susan ministered to her beloved father day and night, his health declined.

On February 14, 1869, Isaac Roop died of pneumonia. He would have turned forty-seven years

Isaac Roop
Courtesy of Lassen County Historical Society

old on his birthday the following month. Newspapers far and wide published the news of Isaac's death. The first provisional Governor of the Nevada Territory and founder of Susanville had succumbed to illness.

Grief stricken, Susan managed to make final arrangements with the help of her husband. Isaac was laid to rest in the Susanville Cemetery on a beautiful knoll above town, on the very same land that he had donated to the community in 1860. Isaac was never reunited with his sons. The last time he saw them was in September of 1850 when Isaiah was four and John was six years old.

Alexander's days as a teamster came to an end, as he desired to work in Susanville and remain close to the family who needed him. A.T. took over

Alexander (A.T.) Arnold and Susan E. Roop Arnold
*Courtesy of History of the State of California
and Biographical Record of the Sierras*

management of the town water system after Isaac's passing. Two years before his death, Isaac had granted the Roop Water Ditches to his son, John V. Roop of Keokuk County, Iowa, and daughter, Susan E. Arnold of Lassen County.

In a state of deep mourning, Susan secluded herself in her home while she cared for her children, little Susan, who was almost three years old, and baby Isaac Arnold, six months old.

Susan's family travels mirrored the migration patterns of pioneers during the nineteenth century. The Roop, Gardner, and Arnold families all pushed the boundaries, moving farther west with each generation. From Pennsylvania to Ohio, and on to California during the Gold Rush, Susan's extended family members were pioneer settlers in the open and fertile lands of the West. They were not afraid to be the first to settle in regions they had never seen, as they hoped to attain a better life for themselves and for their descendants.

A dedicated wife, mother, and daughter, Susan spent her lifetime caring for the family she loved in the town named in her honor.

Many hard-working emigrants, who together established a permanent community along the Nobles Immigrant Trail, settled the town of Susanville.

Susanville's Main Street was an important thoroughfare when Susan arrived in 1863. It remains so today, over one hundred and fifty years later.

The Roops, The Arnolds & A Girl Named Susan

SUSANVILLE

Epilogue

Susan and Alexander would have six more children in the years that followed, although not all would survive them. The Arnold's remained a devoted couple, married just two months short of fifty years. They spent their lives active in church and community affairs, in an effort to ensure their children would have a happy and promising future.

Alexander Thrall Arnold

Alexander and Susan Arnold were married for nearly fifty years. Alexander died on October 23, 1914, at the age of eighty-one, just two months short of his golden wedding anniversary. Alexander managed the town water system after the death of his father-in-law. He was engaged in several occupations during his lifetime including: waterworks manager, teamster, livery, farming, dairy, and a shoe business in Susanville. He was a member of Lassen Lodge #149 for fifty-one years and was a Master Mason. He is buried in the Susanville Cemetery.

Alexander was a member of the Lassen County Pioneer Society, which was organized in 1882. The group was open to members who established residence in the valley before July 1, 1860. There were some exceptions with membership approval. John Garrett and Robert Moody who had moved to the area after 1860, were allowed to join the group.

Lassen County Pioneer Society
Back Row left to right: John Garrett, Wright P. Hall, John C. Davis, Abraham L. Tunicon, Ephraim V. Spencer, William B. Long, Thomas Montgomery, Dr. Robert Moody.
Front Row left to right: Robert Johnston, Loyal Woodstock, Frank S. Strong, William H. Jenison, Frank Thomas, Alexander T. Arnold,
Eber C. Bangham.
Courtesy of Lassen County Historical Society

SUSANVILLE

Leroy Dell Arnold

Alexander's oldest son, Leroy Dell Arnold (who had been born before A. T.'s marriage to Susan) moved to Susanville in 1876 when he was twenty-two. He spent his years working at the planing mill located on the Susan River near the Richmond Road Bridge. He passed away on June 1, 1913 at the age of fifty-nine, one year before his father died. Leroy is buried in the Susanville Cemetery.

Arnold Planing Mill
Courtesy of Lassen County Historical Society

Susan Roop Arnold

During Susan and Alexander's marriage, they were blessed with eight children. Five children survived them. Five years after the Arnold's second child, Isaac, was born, they had two more sons, born a year apart. Both died in infancy from childhood illnesses. When four more children arrived over the course of the next eleven years, the Arnold house was full of children's laughter.

Susan and Alexander suffered the loss of a third child in 1898. Their seventeen-year-old son, Mark had been working at Hayden Hill hauling timber and supplies when he fell ill. Hayden Hill was a small mining town located roughly sixty miles northwest of Susanville. A call had gone out for wagon drivers, and Mark Arnold had hired on, eager to earn a wage.

He traveled to Hayden Hill for work and found a small mining town occupied with townsfolk, miners, houses, hotels, a schoolhouse, post office, store, saloon, and blacksmith shop. When he became ill, the residents of Hayden Hill comforted Mark until his parents were able to take him home to Susanville to care for him. Although he was a fit and vigorous young man, Mark succumbed to appendicitis, and died on May 7, 1898.

The children of Susan and Alexander Arnold:

SUSANVILLE

1. Susan M. Arnold b. June 21, 1866 d. November 27, 1937.

2. Isaac Newton Arnold b. August 23, 1868 d. February 16, 1938.

3. Alexander Thrall Arnold Jr. b. October 12, 1873 d. March 1, 1874.

4. Thomas Cutler Arnold b. December 23, 1874 d. April 17, 1875.

5. Dora Mary Arnold b. May 13, 1876 d. December 21, 1921.

6. Carl Victor Arnold b. May 24, 1879 d. June 24, 1951.

7. Mark Eugene Arnold b. October 17, 1881 d. May 7, 1898.

8. Medford "Med" Roop Arnold b. January 25, 1885 d. June 16, 1967.

In 1870 the Arnold's lived on Main Street in the home that was referred to as the Roop House. After Isaac's death it was referred to as the Arnold House. Near the Arnold's home were merchants: a retail store, bookseller, butcher shop, drugstore, hotel and stage stop, as well as several wash houses.

The 1870 U.S. Federal Census for Susanville, Lassen County, California listed this information:

Constantia Anna Theodosia Hall, left
Marietta "Mollie Stiles Hall, center
Susan Roop Arnold, right
about 1910
Courtesy of Lassen County Historical Society

SUSANVILLE

A.T. Arnold, gardener, age 37; S.E. Arnold, wife, age 26; S.M. Arnold, age 4; I.N. Arnold, age 1.

A.T. Arnold, value of real estate $5,000, value of personal estate $900.

Ten years later, the 1880 Susanville Census enumerated on the 9th of June. Alex T. Arnold was listed as head of household, a fruit grower.

In the home was Susan Arnold his wife, a housekeeper, children Susan and I.N. Arnold who attended school, and two younger children, Dora and Carl Victor Arnold. Alexander's oldest son, Leroy was a near neighbor.

The 1880 U.S. Federal Census Susanville, Lassen County, California included these details:

Alex T. Arnold, age 48; Susan E. Arnold, age 38; Susan M. Arnold, age 14; I.N. Arnold, age 11; Dora M. Arnold, age 4; Victor Arnold, age 1.

L. D. Arnold, laborer, age 27; Estella Arnold, wife, age 22; Ezra Arnold, son. age 1; Ezra Soule, father-in-law, wagon maker, age 52; Jesse Soule, sister-in-law, age 23; Minnie Spencer, cousin, age 10.

A widow for nearly seven years, Susan died on July 22, 1921 at the age of seventy-nine. She is buried next to her husband in the Susanville Cemetery.

Dr. John V. Roop standing on the right
(Man on left is unknown)
Courtesy of Lassen County Historical Society

SUSANVILLE

John Valentine Roop

Susan's brother, John, had two horses shot out from under him during the four years of Civil War battles he endured. The Grand Army man served under both General Grant and General Sherman. He had no less than seven bullets pass through his clothing, but was wounded only once, which was on the March to the Sea.

John Roop and Elenora Halferty were married immediately following the end of the Civil War. Their four children were born in Iowa. The family spent at least twelve years there before moving to Nebraska.

The 1880 U.S. Federal Census Sicily, in Gage County, Nebraska lists the following information:

> John V. Roop, physician, age 36; Elenora H. Roop, wife, age 35; Loveln Arnold, age 14; Columbus Arnold, age 10; Mary Arnold, age 6; Scott Arnold, age 3.

In September of 1889, country doctor John Roop of Blue Springs, Nebraska, visited his sister and her family in Susanville. Following a subsequent visit to Susanville twenty years later, in 1919, Dr. John Roop became ill. He died on October 11, 1919 in Daugherty, Murray County, Oklahoma at the age of seventy-five.

The Gardners

John Garner, Jr. and David Gardner

In 1870, Susan's uncles John and David Gardner lived next door to each other in the city of Ottawa, in LaSalle County, Illinois. Susan had lived with her uncles and grandparents for thirteen years after Isaac departed for California. Although David Gardner was her uncle, he was the same age as Susan and, being raised together, they were much like siblings.

By 1870 Susan's grandmother, Jane Gardner was a widow. She lived first with her son David, and then with her older son John, Jr. in Illinois.

The 1870 U. S. Federal Census Ottawa, LaSalle County Illinois lists these details:

> David Gardner, carriage maker, age 28;
> Sara Gardner, wife, age 21; Lulu Gardner,
> 8 months; Jane Gardner, age 71.
> John Gardner, carriage maker, age 40;
> Lucy Gardner, wife, age 36; Virtue
> Gardner, age 13; Frank Gardner, age 10;
> Burton Gardner, age 3.

SUSANVILLE

The Roops

Josiah Roop

Born circa 1817, Maryland. Josiah Roop
married Elizabeth Shafer on November
28, 1837 in Carroll County, Maryland.
Josiah died June 14, 1852 aboard the
SS Prometheus, and was buried at sea.

David Roop

Joseph and Susannah's second son, David
Roop, lived his life in Seneca County, Ohio, with his
family. He died in 1880 at the age of sixty-two.

Born circa 1818, Maryland Died May
4, 1880, buried Dunkard Cemetery,
Bloomville, Seneca County, Ohio.

William H. Roop, son of David and
Elizabeth Roop; Born January 21,
1850, Died March 12, 1872, buried in
the Dunkard Cemetery, Bloomville,
Seneca County, Ohio.

Elizabeth Roop Koller, daughter of David and Elizabeth Roop, Born April 23, 1841, Died October 17, 1921, buried Woodlawn Cemetery, Bloomville, Seneca County, Ohio.

The 1850 U.S. Federal Census Bloom, Seneca, Ohio lists the following information:

David Roop, farmer, age 32; Elizabeth Roop, wife, age 35; Susannah Roop, age 10; Elizabeth Roop, age 18; Josiah Roop, age 7; William. H. Roop, age 0; Elizabeth Hoffman (mother of Elizabeth Roop), age 66.

Twenty years later, the 1870 U.S. Census Bloom, Seneca, Ohio gives these details:

David Roop, farmer, age 52; Elisabeth [Elizabeth] Roop, age 55; William Roop, age 20; Ezra Roop, age 14; Susan E. Roop, age 21.

David Roop, value of real estate $19,000, and the value of personal estate $1,200.

SUSANVILLE

Ephraim Roop

Born circa 1821 in Maryland, died November 28, 1868 on the Isthmus of Panama.

Isaac Roop

Born March 13, 1822, Maryland. Died February 14, 1869 Susanville, California. He is buried in the Susanville Cemetery.

Married Nancy Gardner December 24, 1840.

Children: Susan Engle Roop, Born November 13, 1841; John Valentine Roop, Born November 27, 1843; Isaiah Brian Roop, Born November 30, 1845.

Israel Roop

Israel Roop was a year younger than Isaac and spent his life in Seneca County, Ohio. Israel lived a long life and died at the age of eighty-one.

Born September 23, 1823, Maryland. Died May 6, 1904, buried in Dunkard Cemetery, Bloom Community Grange, Seneca County, Ohio.

Mary Roop, wife of Israel, born August 3, 1821, Ohio. Died August 6, 1880, buried Dunkard Cemetery, Bloomville, Seneca County, Ohio.

Children: Emiline Roop, born 1844; Eliza Roop, born 1846; Ida Roop, born 1849; Clara Roop, born 1853; Jesse Roop, born 1858.

Eliza J. Roop, born June 26, 1846, daughter of Israel and Mary Roop, died June 13, 1869, buried Dunkard Cemetery, Bloomville, Seneca County, Ohio.

The 1850 U.S. Federal Census Bloom Township, Seneca, Ohio provided the following:

Israel Roop, merchant, age 27; Mary Roop, wife, age 28; Emiline [Emmaline] Roop, age 6; Eliza J. Roop, age 4; Samuel Ingle, age 28.

Twenty years later, the 1870 U.S. Federal Census Reed, Seneca, Ohio showed this:

Isearel [Israel] Roop, farmer, age 46; Mary Roop, age 48; Emmaline Roop, age 26; Clara Roop, age 17; Jesse

Roop, age 12; Ella Wood, age 12; Alex McIntrick age 18.

Israel Roop, value of real estate $9,000, value of personal estate $3,200.

Ten years following, the 1880 U.S. Federal Census Attica, Seneca, Ohio gave these details:

Israel Roop, age 56; Mary Roop, age 59; Clara Roop, teacher, age 27; Jesse Roop, clothing and dry goods, age 22; Ella Wood, niece, age 22.

John Roop

John Roop spent his life in Keokuk County, Iowa. He lived near his parents, Joseph and Susannah Roop. John died at the age of seventy-nine in 1904, the same year that his brother Israel passed away.

John Roop, born June 25, 1825, Maryland. Died August 9, 1904, buried Halferty Cemetery, Keokuk County, Iowa.

John Roop married Elizabeth Sherraden November 26, 1846 in Ashland County, Ohio, daughter Susan Roop,* born circa 1848, the family moved to Iowa by 1850.

* Niece of Isaac Roop.

Elizabeth Sherraden Roop, born circa 1826, died March 15, 1850, buried Friends Cemetery in Richland, Keokuk County, Iowa*

John Roop and daughter, Susan lived with Elizabeth's family after her death.

The 1850 U.S. Census District 26, Keokuk, Iowa listed this information:

> Oliver Sheraden, a merchant, age 35; Lydia Sheraden, wife, age 28; Charles Sheraden, age 4; Emma Sheraden, age 2; John Roop, age 23; Susan Roop, age 2.

John married a second time to Delilah Brolliar in Iowa. Delilah born February 15, 1830, died August 24, 1904, buried Halferty Cemetery, Keokuk County, Iowa.

Ten years later, the 1860 U.S. Federal Census Jackson, Keokuk, Iowa showed:

> John Roop, farmer, age 35; Delilah Roop, age 30; Susan E. Roop, age 12; Joseph W. Roop, age 7; Mary A. Roop, age 5; Martha F. Roop, Arthur W. Roop, age 11 months.

> John Roop, value of real estate $2,000, value of personal estate $450.

---

* The surname Sheridan, was written with various spellings in census documents: Sheradan, Sheraden, Sherraden

SUSANVILLE

Eli Roop

Infant, died at two months of age.

Jonas Roop

Jonas Engle Roop was the eighth child, the eighth son, born to Joseph and Susannah Roop. Following his overland adventure to Shasta in 1852, when he was twenty-four, Jonas returned home to Ohio in 1853. The following spring he settled in Lucas County, Ohio, and married Margaret Allen. The two had become acquainted before his journey to California. The newlyweds settled in Ohio where Jonas practiced medicine. He was a well-respected physician and professor at Physio-Medical College in Cincinnati.

Jonas and Margaret moved to the country near Ashland when the health of their youngest child, Henry began to suffer. They had lost their first four children to illnesses and an accident, and were understandably protective of their remaining child.

Dr. Jonas Roop lived a long and successful life, active in the medical profession. After Margaret's death, Jonas and their son Henry, who was also a physician, lived together in Chicago.

Jonas Roop, born September 25, 1828 in Maryland. Died after 1910, in Illinois. Jonas Roop married Margaret Allen of Lucas County, Ohio on May 31, 1854. They had five children. Edward died of cholera at the age of six months; Jonas Wilber Roop, born March 7, 1863, died at the age of five months on August 7, of general weakness, buried Dunkard Cemetery, Bloomville, Seneca County, Ohio; Cora Bell Roop, died at the age of ten months of cholera; George Joseph Roop, born 1855 drowned on June 1, 1868, aged thirteen years; Henry Roop, born 1870.

The 1870 U.S. Federal Census Morrow, Warren, Ohio reported:

Jonas E. Roop, physician, age 41; Margaret A. Roop, age 35; Henry S. Roop, age 3 months; Melissa Wilkins, domestic servant, age 20.

Forty years later, the 1910 U.S. Federal Census Chicago Ward 13, Cook, Illinois gave these details:

Jonas E. Roop, physician, widowed, age 81; Henry T. Roop, son, physician, age 40; Etta Joyce, servant, age 49; Elva Maybee, boarder, age 26.

Elizabeth Roop

Born July 17, 1832 in Maryland, died May 2, 1865, buried Dunkard Cemetery Bloomville, Seneca County, Ohio.

SUSANVILLE

Mary Jane Roop

Mary Jane was the tenth child born to Joseph and Susannah Roop. She was married to Thomas Calhoun, nine years her senior, who was a farmer. They spent their lives in Ashland County, Ohio. Thomas and Mary Jane had seven children: Alexander, James, John, Jennie, Howard, Frank, and Ettie Calhoun. In her later years, when Mary Jane Calhoun was a widow, she lived with her son, Frank at number 10 Main Street in the village of Savannah, Ohio.

> Mary Jane Roop, born March 9, 1833, Maryland. Died 1918 Ashland, Ohio.
> Mary Jane Roop married Thomas Calhoun March 7, 1850, Ashland County, Ohio.

The 1860 U.S. Census Orange Township, Ashland County, Ohio showed these details:

> Thomas Calhoun, farmer, age 35, born Ireland; Mary J. Calhoun, wife, age 27; Alexander Calhoun, age 8; James Calhoun, age 6; Mary Calhoun, age 2; John Calhoun, age 1.

Ten years later, the 1870 U.S. Federal Census Orange Township, Ashland, Ohio gave this information:

> Thomas Calhoun, farmer, age 45; Mary
> J. Calhoun, wife, age 37; Alexander
> Calhoun, age 18; James Calhoun,
> age 16; John Calhoun, age 11; Jennie
> Calhoun, age 8; Howard Calhoun, age
> 3; Frank Calhoun, age six months.

> Thomas Calhoun, value of real estate
> $8,000, value of personal estate $1,200.

Forty years after the 1870 census, the 1910
U.S. Federal Census Clear Creek, Ashland, Ohio had
this information:

> Mary J. Calhoun, widowed age 77;
> Frank Calhoun, son age 40.

Joseph N. Roop

Joseph was the youngest of Isaac Roop's
siblings. In 1863, at the age of twenty-seven, Joseph
N. Roop married Julia Ann Myers, age twenty-five.
Joseph N. and Julia had two children, John and Ida
Roop. Joseph N. was a butcher by trade, and the
family lived on Orange Street in the city of Ashland
when the census was enumerated on June 19, 1880.

In March of 1883, Joseph N. and his family
sold their property in Ashland County, Ohio. They

SUSANVILLE

moved to Williamsport in the Dakota Territory, along with several other families from the Ashland area.

Together the Ashland folks helped to form the county of Emmons in the Dakota Territory. Joseph N. Roop was elected Emmons County Treasurer. On August 21, 1884 he was appointed as the postmaster of Roop Post Office in Emmons County.

Following is information recorded about Roop Post Office:

> Official Register of the United States, Federal Employees, July 1, 1895 Post Office: Roop. County: Emmons. Postmaster: Joseph N. Roop Compensation $154.31.

Joseph N. died in 1906 and was predeceased in death by his daughter, Mary Ida Roop Savage in 1902. Both are buried in the Roop Cemetery south of Braddock. His wife Julia moved to Bismarck after the death of her husband.

> Joseph N. Roop, born January 1836, Maryland. Died 1906 Emmons County, North Dakota, buried Roop Cemetery south of Braddock.

> Joseph N. Roop married Julia Ann Myers November 25, 1863 Ashland County, Ohio.

Julia Roop, wife of Joseph N. Roop, born September 7, 1838, died May 24, 1917, buried Hazelton Cemetery, Emmons County, North Dakota.

Following is information contained in the 1870 U.S. Federal Census Ashland, Ashland, Ohio:

Joseph [N.] Roop, grocer, age 34; Julia Roop, age 33; John Roop, age 5; Mary I. Roop, age 1; Hannah Myers, age 72; Barbara Farmer, age 38.

The census ten years later in 1880 U.S. Federal Census Ashland, Ashland, Ohio gave these details:

Joseph [N.] Roop, butcher, age 44; Julia Roop, age 42; John Roop, age 15; Ida M. Roop, age 11.

After the family moved to the Dakota Territory, the 1900 U.S. Federal Census Logan, Emmons, North Dakota showed:

Joseph [N.] Roop, farmer, age 64; Julia Roop, wife, age 61; Barbara Farmer, servant, age 62.

SUSANVILLE

The Arnolds

Cutler Arnold

Alexander's oldest brother, Cutler, was a pioneer settler in California, who went west during the Gold Rush in 1849. An industrious man with a large family, Cutler spent the first five years in California working as a farmer, freighter, and merchant. He moved to Rooptown in 1857 and built the town's first log hotel.

For the next eleven years, Cutler and his wife, Emily Arnold, raised eight children in Rooptown, later named Susanville. In 1868 the family moved to San Buenaventura, taking up large plot of land. Cutler died on October 16, 1892 at the age of seventy-three, a pioneer settler in Ventura County.

Cutler Arnold married Emily Huff on October 16, 1841 Illinois.

The 1860 U.S. Federal Census Honey Lake Valley, Plumas, California, listed:

> Cutler Arnold, farmer, age 41; Emily Arnold, wife, age 41; Henry Arnold, age 21; Leroy Arnold, age 18; Matthew Arnold, age 16; Eugene Arnold, age 14; Edward Arnold, age 6; Eunice Arnold, age 3; George Arnold, age 1.

> Cutler Arnold, value of real estate $3,000, value of personal estate $1,200.

The 1880 U.S. Federal Census Hueneme, Ventura, California showed members of the extended Arnold family:

Cutler Arnold, farmer, age 62; Emily Arnold, wife, age 60; George Arnold, age 21; Fanny Arnold, age 16; T. Blee, employee, age 22; John Hough, employee, age 19; Charles Pitcher, son-in-law, age 23; Emma Eunice (Arnold) Pitcher, daughter, age 20; Annie Bland, boarder, age 20.

Henry Arnold, farmer, age 41; Pamelia Arnold, wife, age 31; Charles Arnold, age 13; Anna Arnold, age 11; Suzie age 3. Leroy Arnold, farmer, age 37; Caroline Arnold, wife, age 33; Effie Arnold, age 13; Mary Arnold, age 11; Martha Arnold, age 6; Olive Arnold, age 3; Cutler Arnold, age 6 months; Charles Journigan, employee, age 19.

Matthew Arnold, farmer, age 35; Eliza Arnold, wife, age 24; Ralph Arnold, age 2; Frank Shrode, employee, age 22.

Eugene Arnold, farmer, age 33; Belle H. Arnold, wife, age 20; Floyd Arnold, age 1; M. Adeline Hawkins, sister-in-law, age 13.

Edward F. Arnold, farmer, age 25; Lou Anna Arnold, wife, age 28; Walter

Arnold, age 1; Lora Arnold, age 1 month.

Leroy Nathan Arnold

Leroy served as a private in the Mexican War. After his discharge in 1848, he traveled to California during the Gold Rush of 1849. Leroy spent his life prospecting. His wife, Mariah, left for Siskiyou County, and remarried in 1866. She took their small children, Katherine and Frank with her.

In his later years, Leroy traveled between Susanville and Winnemucca. In 1900, at the age of seventy-six, he was admitted to the Sawtelle Old Soldiers Home in Los Angeles County. On the intake papers, he listed his closest relative as his son, Frank Arnold of Fort Jones, Siskiyou County California. Leroy died of exhaustion at the age of seventy-seven on November 19, 1901. He is buried in Los Angeles National Cemetery.

The 1870 U.S. Federal Census Scott Valley, Siskiyou, California, listed the following:

A. Bowers, miner, age 40; Maria Bowers, wife, age 26; Kate (Arnold) Bowers, age 9; Frank (Arnold) Bowers, age 7; Emma Bowers, age 4; Willard Bowers, age 3; Walter Bowers, age 1.

The 1882 California Voters Register, Susanville, Lassen, California lists:

Leroy N. Arnold, miner, age 58.

The 1900 U.S. Federal Census Winnemucca, Humboldt, Nevada gives this:

Leroy Arnold, age 75. Dwelling 299 Bridge Street, Winnemucca.

SUSANVILLE

Susan Roop Arnold
Courtesy of Lassen Historical Society

SUSANVILLE

Important Dates
in Susan Roop's Timeline

December 24, 1840 Isaac Newton Roop and Nancy Gardner were married

November 13, 1841 Susan Engle Roop was born, Ashland County, Ohio

November 27, 1843 John Valentine Roop was born, Ashland County, Ohio

November 30, 1845 Isaiah Brian Roop was born, Ashland County, Ohio

May 23, 1850 Nancy Gardner Roop died of typhoid fever

September 9, 1850 Isaac Roop departed New York for California via Panama

October 18, 1850 Isaac Roop arrived in San Francisco on the steamer *Oregon*

November 4, 1850 Isaac joined his brother Josiah Roop in Shasta

March 18, 1852 Ephraim and Jonas Roop departed Ohio overland to California

May 8, 1852 Josiah Roop departed for Ohio via Nicaragua

June 14, 1852 Josiah Roop died of dysentery and was buried at sea

September 9, 1852 Ephraim and Jonas Roop arrived in California via wagon train

1852 Isaac Roop was appointed Postmaster in Shasta

June 14, 1853 Fire destroyed the town of Shasta and most of Isaac Roop's possessions

September 1853 Isaac Roop arrived in Honey Lake Valley

June 1854 Isaac Roop built trading post assisted by his brother Ephraim Roop

1856 John Roop moved from Ohio to Iowa with his Roop grandparents

1857 Susan Roop moved to Wayne County Ohio with her Gardner grandparents

April 1858 Isaac named the town Susanville, in honor of his daughter Susan Roop

1858 Alexander Arnold moved to Susanville

September 7, 1859 Isaac Roop was elected Provisional Governor of Nevada Territory

June 11, 1861 Isaiah Brian Roop enlisted in the Twenty Third Ohio Infantry

SUSANVILLE

July 11, 1861 John Valentine Roop enlisted in the Seventh Iowa Infantry

September 17, 1862 Isaiah Roop lost his right arm at the battle of Antietam

November 13, 1862 Susan Roop turned twenty-one years old

November 21, 1862 Susan Roop boarded the steamer Champion in New York

December 2, 1862 Susan Roop departed Panama on the steamer Orizaba

December 16, 1862 Isaac Roop attended the legislative session in Carson City

December 18, 1862 Susan Roop arrived in San Francisco

December 26, 1862 Susan Roop arrived in Carson City

January 1863 Susan and Isaac Roop arrived in Susanville

February 15, 1863 the Sagebrush War

February 24, 1864 Isaiah Roop, age eighteen, died of smallpox in Trenton, Ohio

December of 1864 John Roop wounded on the march through Georgia

December 27, 1864 Susan Engle Roop married Alexander Thrall Arnold

May 24. 1865 John Roop at Grand Review in Washington D.C.

August 21, 1865 John Roop married Elenora Halferty in Iowa

November 28, 1868 Ephraim Roop died of smallpox in Panama

February 14, 1869 Isaac Roop died of pneumonia in Susanville

October 23, 1914 Alexander Thrall Arnold died in Susanville at the age of eighty-one

July 22, 1921 Susan Roop died in Susanville at the age of seventy-nine

SUSANVILLE

Acknowledgments

I began research on the life of Susan Roop after questioning why there was not a book written about her. After all, she is our town's namesake. I decided to put my own pen to paper and started to document the life of the only daughter of Nevada Territory's Provisional Governor.

I began with an outline, believing I would publish a brief biography with a few photos, names, and dates. The book began to take on a life of its own as I uncovered more and more interesting facts, not only about Susan's family but about life in the settlement years of northeastern California. It has taken three years of research and writing to complete this manuscript for publication.

I would like to thank Mary Hasselwander who first reviewed the draft. A huge thank you to Jo Massey Johnston, friend and author who spent countless hours on the final edit. She has shared her knowledge of writing, editing, and publishing, for which I am grateful.

Thanks to Annette Chaudet at Pronghorn Press for her interest and help with the project.

And special thanks to my husband, Tony Jonas, former president of the Lassen County Historical Society, who assisted with research and documentation.

Sandra Jonas pictured in front of Roop's Fort 2013
Courtesy of the Author

SUSANVILLE

About The Author

Sandra Jonas lives with her husband Tony in Susanville, California. She reenacts the life of Susan Roop Arnold at local events. Sandra is a member of the Lassen County Historical Society and volunteers at the museum. Her interest in women's history during the settlement of the West, prompted Sandra to document the life of Susan Roop Arnold

The Roops, The Arnolds & A Girl Named Susan

SUSANVILLE

Appendix A

Josiah and Isaac's properties in the Old Town of Shasta:

Josiah and Isaac both invested heavily in the mercantile store on Main Street. In March of 1853 it was sold.

Josiah owned the building that housed the Post Office next to the Empire Hotel on Main Street. On June 15, 1853 it burned down.

Old Dominion House (Hotel) on Main Street. Isaac invested with Josiah. In March of 1853 it was appraised at $4,000. On June 15, 1853 it burned down.

Oak Bottom House, nine miles west of Shasta. Josiah bought it September 8, 1851 and sold it on March 5, 1852 for $912.

July 6, 1852 Isaac purchased a lot in the town of Shasta. He sold it on January 17, 1854 for $500.

November 1852 Isaac sold Josiah's half interest in a corral located in the town of Shasta for $280.

December 1852 Isaac purchased seventy acres of land two miles east of Shasta.

Isaac sold Josiah's house and lot in 1853 for $2,000.

The Roops, The Arnolds & A Girl Named Susan

SUSANVILLE

Bibliography

Books

Brock, Richard and Robert Black. *A Guide to the Nobles Trail*. Reno, NV: Trails West, Inc., 2008.

Butler, James Thomas. *Isaac Roop: Pioneer & Political Leader of Northeastern California*. A Lassen County Historical Society Book. Janesville, CA: High Desert Press, 1994.

Davis, William N. Jr. *Sage Brush Corner; the Opening of California's Northeast*. New York and London: Garland Publishing, Inc., 1974.

Encyclopedia Americana - International Edition, Vol. 15. *Iowa*, Danbury, CT: Grolier Incorporated, 1997, 353-355.

Encyclopedia Americana - International Edition, Vol. 20. *Ohio*, Danbury, CT: Grolier Incorporated, 1997, 654-661.

Encyclopedia Americana - International Edition, Vol. 21. *Pennsylvania*, Danbury, CT: Grolier Incorporated, 1997, 639-646.

Fairfield, Asa Merrill. *Fairfield's Pioneer History of Lassen County, California*. San Francisco: Crocker and Company, 1916.

Ward, Geoffrey C., Ken Burns, and Ric Burns. *The Civil War: An Illustrated History*. New York: Knopf, 1990.

Newspapers

Lassen Advocate, "Born," Susanville, CA. 26 December, 1874.
Lassen Advocate, "Was Son of Pioneer," Susanville, CA. 7
        November, 1919.
Sage Brush, "Born," Susanville, CA, 5 September,1868.
Sage Brush, "Sad News," Susanville, CA. 16 January, 1869.
Sage Brush, "Resolution on the Death of I. N. Roop,"
        Susanville, CA. 20 February, 1869.
Sage Brush, "Obituary," Susanville, CA. 20 February, 1869.

Online Sources - Ancestry:

All of the following references are from Ancestry.com
http://home.ancestry.com. Provo, UT, USA: Ancestry.
com Operations, Inc. Each entry includes title, location of
material, date, followed by date the file was accessed. All
are listed in alphabetical order.

1820 U.S. Census; Census Place: Westminster,
        Frederick, Maryland; Page: *199;* NARA Roll:
        M33-43; M33_43; Image: *202. Joseph Roop.* 2010.
        12 October 2013.
1830 U.S. Census; Census Place: District 7, Frederick,
        Maryland; Page: *221;* NARA Series: *M19;* Roll
        Number: *57;* Family History Film: *0013180.*
        Joseph Roop. 2010. 13 October 2013.
1840 U.S. Census Place: Bloom, Seneca,
        Ohio; Roll: *426;* Page: *138;* Image: *282;* Family
        History Library Film: *0020176. Josiah Roop.* 2010.
        1 September 2013.
1840 U.S. Census Place: Montgomery, Richland, Ohio;
        Roll: *423;* Page: *24;* Image: *52;* Family   History
        Library Film: *0020175. John Gardner.* 2010. 14
        August 2013.

SUSANVILLE

1850 U.S. Census Place: Bloom, Seneca,
    Ohio; Roll: *M432_728;* Page: *144B; Image: 663.*
    David Roop. 2009. 23 November 2013.
1850 U.S. Census Place: Bloom, Seneca, Ohio
    Roll: *M432_728;* Page: *144A; Image: 662. Israel*
    Roop. 2009. 23 November 2013.
1850 U.S. Census Place: District 26, Keokuk,
    Iowa; Roll: *M432_185;* Page: *226B;* Image: 457
    John Roop. 2009. 5 April 2014.
1850 U.S. Census Place: Montgomery, Ashland, Ohio;
    Roll: *M432_658;* Page: *451A;* Image:*145. Isaiah*
    Roop. 2009. 7 September 2013.
1850 U.S. Census Place: Montgomery, Ashland, Ohio;
    Roll: *M432_658;* Page: *450B;* Image *144. John*
    Gardner. 2009. 7 September 2013.
1850 U.S. Census Place: Montgomery, Ashland, Ohio;
    Roll: *M432_658;* Page: *452B;* Image: *151. John*
    Roop. 2009. 7 September 2013.
1850 U.S. Census Place: Montgomery, Ashland, Ohio;
    Roll: *M432_658;* Page: *452B; Image: 148. Joseph*
    Roop. 2009. 7 September 2013.
1850 U.S. Census Place: Montgomery, Ashland,
    Ohio; Archive Collection Number: *T1159;*
    Roll: *1;* Line: *39;* Schedule Type: *Joseph Roop,*
    Agriculture. 2009. 22 March 2014.
1850 U.S. Census Place: Peru, Morrow, Ohio; Roll:
    M432_716; Page: *66A; Image: 503. Nathan*
    Arnold. 2009. 22 November 2014.
1850 U.S. Census Place: Samonauk, DeKalb, Illinois;
    Roll: *M432_104;* Page: *337B; Image: 347.*
    Cutler Arnold. 2009. 1 November 2014.
1850 U.S. Census Place: Scipio, Seneca, Ohio; Roll:
    M432_728; Page: *26A; Image: 426. Elizabeth Roop.*
    17 December 2015.

1850 U.S. Census Place: Shasta, Shasta, California; Roll: *M432_35;* Page: *333A;* Image: *648. Josiah Roop.* 2009. 13 April 2014.

1860 U.S. Census Place: Canaan, Wayne, Ohio; Roll: *M653_1051;* Page: *247;* Image: *81;* Family History Library Film: *805051. John Gardner.* 2009. 31 May 2014.

1860 U.S. Census Place: Honey Lake Valley, Plumas, California; Roll: *M653_62;* Page: *979;* Image: *421;* Family History Library Film: *803062. Cutler Arnold.* 2009. 22 November 2014.

1860 U.S. Census Place: Honey Lake Valley, Plumas, California; Roll: *M653_62;* Page: *981;* Image: *423;* Family History Library Film: *803062. Leroy Arnold.* 2009. 22 November 2014.

1860 U.S. Census Place: Jackson, Keokuk, Iowa; Roll: *M653_329;* Page: *878;*Image: *142;* Family History Library Film: *803329. John Roop, Joseph Roop* 2009. 24 May 2014.

1860 U.S. Census Place: Jackson, Keokuk, Iowa; Roll: *M653_329;* Page: *868;* Image: *132;* Family History Library Film: *803329. Paul Sheraden.* 2009. 24 May 2014.

1860 U.S. Census Place: Orange, Ashland, Ohio; Roll: *M653_930;* Page: *46;* Image: *95;* Family History Library Film: *803930. Mary Roop Calhoun.* 2009. 5 October 2014.

1860 U.S. Census Place: Reed, Seneca, Ohio; Roll: *M653_1034;* Page: *143;* Image: *292;* Family History Library Film: *805034. Israel Roop.* 2009. 5 October 2014.

1860 U.S. Census Place: Tipton, Cedar, Iowa; Roll: *M653_314;* Page: *30;* Image: *30;* Family History Library Film: *803314. Kate Arnold.* 2009. 22 November 2015.

SUSANVILLE

1870 U.S. Census Place: Ashland, Ashland, Ohio; Roll: *M593_1169;* Page: *735B;* Image: *328;* Family History Library Film: *552668. John Roop.* 2009. 12 April 2015.

1870 U.S. Census Place: Bloom, Seneca, Ohio; Roll: *M593_1266;* Page: *66A;* Image: *135;* Family History Library Film: *552765. David Roop.* 2009. 30 March 2015.

1870 U.S. Census Place: Jackson, Keokuk, Iowa; Roll: *M593_402;* Page: *335B;* Image: *166;* Family History Library Film: *545901. Joshua White.* 2009. 24 May 2014.

1870 U.S. Census Place: Morrow, Warren, Ohio; Roll: *M593_1277;* Page: *394A;* Image: *395;* Family History Library Film: *552776. Jonas Roop.* 2009. 30 March 2015.

1870 U.S. Census Place: Orange, Ashland, Ohio; Roll: *M593_1169;* Page: *776B;* Image: *410;* Family History Library Film: *552668. Mary Roop Calhoun.* 2009. 5 October 2014.

1870 U.S. Census Place: Ottawa, La Salle, Illinois; Roll: *M593_244;* Page: *604A;* Image: *482;* Family History Library Film: *545743.2009. John Gardner. David Gardner.* 2009. 31 May 2014.

1870 U.S. Census Place: Reed, Seneca, Ohio; Roll: *M593_1266;* Page: *222A;* Image: *448;* Family History Library Film: *552765. Israel Roop.* 2009. 30 March 2015.

1870 U.S. Census Place: Scott Valley, Siskiyou, California; Roll: *M593_89;* Page: *618B;* Image: *556;* Family History Library Film: *545588. Bowers Family, Kate and Frank Arnold.* 2009. 15 August 2015.

1870 U.S. Census Place: Susanville, Lassen, California; Roll: *M593_73;* Page: *441A;* Image: *264;* Family History Library Film: *545572 A.T. Arnold.* 2009. 19 April 2015.

1880 U.S. Census Place: Attica, Seneca, Ohio; Roll:
1066; Family History Film: *1255066;* Page:
389C; Enumeration District: *212;* Image: *0084.*
Israel Roop. 2010. 30 March 2015.
1880 U.S. Census Place: Ashland, Ashland,
Ohio; Roll: *991;* Family History Film:
1254991; Page: *171A;* Enumeration
District: *088;* Image: *0344. Joseph Roop.* 2010.
5 October 2013.
1880 U.S. Census Place: Hueneme, Ventura, California;
Roll: *86;* Family History Film: *1254086;* Page:
260D; Enumeration District: *105;* Image: *0097.*
*2010. Cutler Arnold Family.*2010. 15 August 2015.
1880 U.S. Census Place: Orange, Ashland, Ohio; Roll:
991; Family History Film: *1254991;* Page: *193C;*
Enumeration District: *089;* Image: *0388. Mary*
Jane Calhoun. 2010. 5 April 2015.
1880 U.S. Census Place: Scott Valley, Siskiyou,
California; Roll: *83;* Family History Film:
1254083; Page: *232A;* Enumeration District: *104;*
Image: *0186. Maria Bower.* 2010. 20 February, 2015.
1880 U.S. Census Place: Sicily, Gage, Nebraska; Roll:
749; Family History Film: *1254749;* Page: *104A;*
Enumeration District: *349;* Image: *0455. 2010.*
John V. Roop. 2010. 30 March 2015.
1880 U.S. Census Place: Susanville, Lassen, California;
Roll: *66;* Family History Film:*1254066;* Page: *82D;*
Enumeration District: *053;* Image: *0677 Alex T.*
Arnold. 2010. 19 April 2015.
1880 U.S. Census Place: Susanville, Lassen, California;
Roll: *66;* Family History Film:*1254066;* Page: *82D;*
Enumeration District: *053;* Image: *0677. Leroy*
Dell Arnold. 2010. 19 April 2015.
1882 California, Voter Registers, 1866-1898. Leroy
Arnold. 2011. 12 April 2015.

SUSANVILLE

1884 Appointments of U. S. Postmasters, 1832-1971. Joseph Roop. NARA Microfilm Publication, M841, 145 rolls. Records of the Post Office Department, Record Group Number 28. Washington, D.C.: National Archives. 2010.

1895 U.S. Official Register of the United States, Containing a List of the Officers and Employees in the Civil, Military, and Naval Service 1863-1959. Joseph N. Roop. Department of Commerce and Labor, Bureau of the Census. Digitized books (77 volumes). Oregon State Library, Salem, Oregon. 2014. 5 April 2015.

1900 U.S. Census Place: Logan, Emmons, North Dakota; Roll: *1228;* Page: *2B;* Enumeration District: *0051;* FHL microfilm: *1241228. Joseph Roop.* 2004. 1 3 April 2014.

1900 Census Place: Winnemucca, Humboldt, Nevada; Roll: *943;* Page: *10B;* Enumeration District: *0017;* FHL microfilm: *1240943. Leroy Arnold.* 2011. April 2015.

1900 U.S. National Homes for Disabled Volunteer Soldiers, 1866-1938. Leroy Arnold. 2007. 18 April, 2015.

1901 U.S., Burial Registers, Military Posts and National Cemeteries, 1862-1960. Leroy Nathan Arnold. 2012. 18 April 2015.

1910 U S Census Place: Chicago Ward 13, Cook, Illinois; Roll: *T624_254;* Page: *9B;* Enumeration District: *0632;* FHL microfilm: *1374267. Jonas Roop.* 2006. 9 March 2014.

1910 U.S. Census Place: Clear Creek, Ashland, Ohio; Roll: *T624_1151;* Page: *7A;* Enumeration District: *0001;* FHL microfilm: *1375164. Mary J. Calhoun.* 2006. 30 March 2015.

Illinois Marriages to 1850. Cutler Arnold, Emily Huff 1841. Dodd, Jordan. Original data: Electronic transcription of marriage records held by the individual counties in Illinois. 1997. 15 August 2015.

Iowa Select Marriages, 1809-1992. Index only: *John Roop and Elenora Halferty August 21, 1865.* 2013. 16 February 2015.

Iowa, State Census Collection, 1856, 1885, 1895, 1905, 1915, 1925, as well various special censuses from 1836-1897 obtained from the State Historical Society of Iowa via Heritage Quest. *John Roop, Joseph Roop, Paul Sheraden.* 2010. 17 May 2014.

Pennsylvania, Septennial Census, 1779-1863. John Gardner. 2012. 13 October 2013. *U.S. Appointments of U. S. Postmasters, 1832-1971.* Original data: *Record of Appointment of Postmasters, 1832-1971.* NARA Microfilm Publication, *M841, 145 rolls. Records of the Post Office Department, Record Group Number 28.* Washington, D.C.: National Archives. 2010. 21 June 2014.

U.S. Civil War Draft Registrations Records, 1863-1865. David Roop, Ephraim Roop, Isaac Roop, Israel Roop. Original data: *Consolidated Lists of Civil War Draft Registrations, 1863- 1865.* NM-65, entry 172, 620 volumes. ARC ID: 4213514. Records of the Provost Marshal General's Bureau (Civil War), Record Group 110. National Archives at Washington D.C., 2010. 19 October 2014.

U.S. Federal Census Mortality Schedules Index, 1850-1880. Elizabeth Roop. 1999. 19 December 2015.

SUSANVILLE

Online Sources - Find A Grave

All of the following references are from Find a Grave. http://www.findagrave. Each entry includes author, name of interred, Memorial number, date, followed by date the file was accessed. All are listed in alphabetical order.

Backes, Brian. *Julia A. Myers Roop.* Memorial #79568548. 30 October 2011. 13 April 2014.

Gathering Roots. *Elizabeth Roop Koller.* Memorial #119004911. 20 October 2012. 12 April 2014.

Long, Douglas. *David Roop.* Memorial #99789537. 29 October 2012. 5 April 2014.

Long, Douglas. *Elizabeth Hoffman Roop.* Memorial #99810124. 29 October 2012. 5 April 2014.

Long, Douglas. *Israel Roop.* Memorial #997819343. 29 October 2012. 5 April 2014.

Long, Douglas. *Mary Roop.* Memorial #99819103. 29 October 2012. 5 April 2014.

Miller, Bill. *Nancy Roop.* Memorial #30267492. 2 October2012. 29 November 2013.

Oudejans, Suzanne. *Delilah Roop.* Memorial #16726237. 20 November 2006. 19 April 2014.

Oudejans, Suzanne. *John Roop.* Memorial #16726224. 20 November 2006. 19 April 2014.

Tipton, Jim. *Elizabeth Roop.* Memorial #99819103. 16 June 2013. 12 April 2014.

Weikle, Jill and Ron. *Eliza J. Roop.* Memorial #100444303. 9 November 2012. 5 April 2014.

Weikle, Jill and Ron. *Elizabeth Roop.* Memorial #100444336. 9 November 2012. 5 April 2014.

Weikle, Jill and Ron. *Jonas Wilber Roop.* Memorial #100444262. 9 November 2012. 5 April 2014.

Weikle, Jill and Ron. *Joseph Roop.* Memorial #100444421. 9 November 2012. 5 April 2014.

Weikle, Jill and Ron. *Susannah Roop.* Memorial
    #100444449. 9 November 2012. 5 April 2014.
Weikle, Jill and Ron. *William H. Roop.* Memorial
    #100444473. 9 November 2012. 5 April 2014.
Wolcott, Brenda. *John F. Roop.* Memorial #112421379. 16
    June 2013. 19 December 2015.

Online Newspaper Archives

Daily Alta California

The following references are from *Daily Alta California*, San Francisco. http://cdnc.ucr.edu. They are arranged in alphabetical order by article title, followed by Volume, Number, Page, and date of publication, followed by date accessed.

"Arrival of the Orizaba." Vol. 14, No. 4684, p 1, 19
    December 1862. 23 August 2014.
"Arrival of the Steamer *Oregon.*" Vol. 2, No. 261, p 2, 19
    October 1850. April 12, 2014.
"Black Rock a Failure." Vol. 20, No. 6548, p 1, 18
    February 1868. 1 March 2015.
"By State Telegraph." Vol. 15, No. 4699, p 1, 5 January
    1863. 20 September 2014.
"By State Telegraph." Vol. 15, No. 5049, p 1, 25 December
    1863. 25 January 2015.
"By State Telegraph." Vol. 16, No. 5411, p 1, 28 December
    1864. 1 March 2015.
"City Items: Russ House Inauguration Dinner." Vol. 14,
    No. 4433, p 1, 10 April 1862. 13 July 1862.
"Colonel Lander's U. S. Wagon Road Expedition." Vol. 12,
    No. 172, p 2, 21 June 1860. 4 July 2014.

SUSANVILLE

"Eastward Bound." Vol. 20, No. 6816, p 1, 14 November 1868. 1 March 2015.

"First Effects of the News." Vol.1, No. 261, p 2, 19 October 1850. April 12, 2014.

"Fort Crook." Vol. 12, No. 207, p 1, 27 July 1860. 14 December 2014.

"Honey Lake Valley." Vol. 9, No. 119, p 1, 30 April 1857. 24 May 2014.

"Honey Lake Valley Indians." Vol. 9, No. 191, p 1, 29 October 1857. 25 May 2014.

"Hostilities in Plumas." Vol. 15, No. 4746, p 1, 21 February 1863. 27 September 2014.

"Immigrants" Vol. 13, No. 4225, p 1, 12 September 1861. 26 December 2014.

"Interior Items." Vol. 16, No. 5104, p 1, 20 February 1864. 19 October 2014.

"Lander's Wagon Road Expedition." Vol. 12, No. 139, p 1, 19 May 1860. 7 December 2014. "Letter From Honey Lake Valley." Vol. 9, No. 194, p 1, 24 July 1857. 24 May 2014.

"Letter from the Humboldt Mines." Vol. 13, No. 4222, p 1, 9 September 1861. 27 December 2014.

"Letter from Lander's Expedition." Vol. 12, No. 243, p 1, 1 September 1860. 26 December 2014.

"Nevada Legislature." Vol. 13, No. 4250, p 1, 8 October 1861. 10 May 2014.

"Nevada State Items. Military Movements." Vol. 18, No. 5934, p 1, 9 June 1866. 22 February, 2015.

"New Immigrant Route." Vol. 3, No. 180, p 2, 29 June 1852. 6 June 2015.

"Passengers." Vol. 3, No. 214, p 2, 3 August 1852. 22 November 2014.

"Proceedings of the Territorial Meeting in Carson Valley." Vol. 9, No. 183, p 2, 21 October 1857. 26 May 2014.

Marysville Daily Appeal

The following references are from *Marysville Daily Appeal.* Marysville, California. http://cdnc. ucr.edu. They are arranged in alphabetical order by article title, followed by Volume, Number, Page, and date of publication, followed by date accessed.

"Ambitious Red Bluff," Vol. I, No. 128, p 4, 19 June 1860. 14 December 2014.

"Born," Vol. XIV, No. 8, p 2, 15 July 1866. 22 February 15.

"By Northern Telegraph, From The Sage Brush," Vol. XIII, No. 132, p 3, 5 June 1866. 28 February 2015.

"Lassen County," Vol. XVIII, No. 54, p 3, 20 July 1866. 2 September 1868. 8 March 2015.

"Marysville," Vol. VIII, No. 148, p 2, 23 December 1863. 25 October 2014.

"Matters in Honey Lake," Vol. VIII, No. 14, p 4, 17 July 1863. 5 October 2014.

"Notice to Subscribers," Vol. VII, No. 2, p 2, 3 January 1863. 27 September 2014.

"Our Sacramento Dispatch. Legislative," Vol. IX, No. 78, p 3, 2 April 1864. 25 October 2014. "Plumas Items," Vol. VIII, No. 75, p 2, 27 September 1863. 14 February 2015.

"Stage Line From California to Idaho!" Vol. XIV, No. 12, p 3, 22 February 2015.

Sacramento Daily Union

The following references are from *Sacramento Daily Union*, Sacramento, CA. http://cdnc.ucr.edu. They are arranged in alphabetical order by article title, followed by Volume, Number, Page, and date of publication, followed by date accessed.

SUSANVILLE

"Advertisements. New Hotel Carson City," Vol. 24, No.
　　3666, p 3, 20 December 1862. 31 August 2014.
"Arrivals of Stock," Vol. 17, No. 2636, p 3, 8 September
　　1859. 16 November 2014.
"Births," Vol. 17, No. 2562, p 2, 13 June 1859. 14 June 2015.
"Boundary Line," Vol. 25, No. 3856, p 2, 31 July 1863.
　　5 October 2014.
"By Telegraph to the Union," Vol. 36, No. 5504, p 3,
　　16 November 1868. 15 March 2015.
"California Legislature," Vol. 23, No. 3427, p 1, 24 March
　　1862. 13 July 2014.
"California Matters," Vol. 15, No. 2241, p 2, 2 June 1858.
　　11 November 2014.
"Death of a Young Patriot," Vol. 27, No. 4117, p 2, 1 June
　　1864. 10 May 2014.
"Difficulties at Honey Lake, The," Vol. 24, No. 3723, p 1.
　　26 February 1863. 27 September 2014.
"From Carson Valley," Vol. 18, No. 2678, p 2, 27 October
　　1859. 16 November 2014.
"From Honey Lake Valley," Volume 12, Number 1746,
　　p 4. 30 October 1856. 24 May 2014.
"From Honey Lake," Vol. 21, No. 3207, p 2, 9 July 1861.
　　1 February 2015.
"From the Interior," Vol. 3, No. 452, p 3, 3 September
　　1852. 19 April 2014.
"From the Interior, Shasta," Vol. V, No. 741, p 3, 9 August
　　1853, 20 April 2014.
"F.W. Lander's Expedition." Vol. 19, No. 2881, p 2, 20 June
　　1860. 20 December 2015.
"Honey Lake." Vol. 14, No. 2173, p 2, 15 March 1858. 26
　　May 2014.
"Honey Lake News," Vol. 18, No. 2728, p 2, 24 December
　　1859. 22 November 2014.
"Indian Affairs," Vol. 14, No. 2060, p 1, 2 November 1857.
　　26 May 2014.

"Indian Valley, Plumas County," Vol. 30, No.4570, p 2,
    14 November 1865. 14 February 2015.
"Items From Humboldt," Vol. 27, No. 4098, p 2, 10 May
    1864. 25 January 2015.
"Letter From Honey Lake Valley," Vol. 11, No. 1701, p 3,
    8 September 1856. 24 May 2014. 30 August 2014.
"Letter From Honey Lake, Susanville," Vol. 23, No. 3562,
    p 4, 28 August 1862. 20 July 2014.
"Letter from Lassen County. Susanville," Vol. 28, No.
    4230, p 5, 11 October 1864. 26 October 2014.
"Letter From Nevada Territory," Vol. 24, No. 3641, p 1,
    21 November 1862. 24 December 2015.
"Letter from the Nevada Territory," Vol. 24, No. 3644,
    p 1, 25 November 1862. 16 August 2014.
"Letter from the Nevada Territory," Vol. 24, No. 3646,
    1, 27 November 1862. 10 August 2014.
"Letter from Nevada Territory," Vol. 24, No. 3655, p 1,
    8 December 1862. 16 August 2014.
"Letter from Nevada Territory," Vol. 24, No. 3668, p 1,
    23 December 1862. 24 August 2014.
"Mail Routes to Honey Lake," Vol. 15, No. 2292, p 1,
    2 August 1858. 11 November 2014.
"Married," Vol. 18, No. 2712, p 2, 6 December 1859.
    22 November 2014.
"Married," Vol. 28, No. 4331, p 2, 7 February 1865.
    14 February 2015.
"Matters in Plumas," Vol. 31, No. 4816, p 3, 4 September
    1866. 22 February 2015.
"Melancholy Death," Vol. 3, No, 432, p 2, 10 August
    1852. 18 April 2014.
"More Emigrants," Vol. 17, No. 2615, p 2, 15 August
    1859. 14 June 2015.
"Mountain Scenery. Ascent of the Sierras, The," Vol. 26,
    No. 3967, p 1, 8 December 1863. 4 October 2014.

SUSANVILLE

"Movements of Ocean Steamers," Vol.3, No. 362, p 2, 19
    May 1852. 17 April 2014.
"News of the Morning," Vol. 23, No. 3427, p 5, 24 March
    1862. 13 July 2014.
"News of the Morning," Vol. 27, No. 4064, p 2, 31 March
    1864. 19 October 2014.
"Ore from the Humboldt," Vol. 21, No. 3252, p 3, 30
    August 1861. 27 December 2014.
"Passengers from the East," Vol. 24, No. 3661, p 2, 15
    December 1862. 23 August 2014.
"Pioneer Stage Company, Advertisement," Vol. 23, No.
    3536, p 4, 29 July 1862.
"Rabbit Creek August 4," Sierra County Correspondence,
    Vol. 9, No. 1363, p 3, 8 August 1855.14 June 2015.
"River Travel," Vol. 19, No. 2899, p 4. 12 July 1860.
    20 July 2014.
"River Travel," Vol. 24, No. 3665, p 4, 19 December 1862.
    24 August 2014.
"Roads Over the Mountains, The," Volu.24, No. 3670,
    p 2, 25 December 1862. 30 August 2014. "Robbers
    North," Vol. 31, No. 4756, p 3, 25 June 1866.
    22 February 2015.
"Shasta," Vol. 5, No. 700, p 2, 21 June 1853. 26 April 2014.
"Sierra Nevada Peaks and Highlands, The," Vol. 25,
    No. 3878, p 1, 26 August 1863. 3 January 2015.
"Small Pox on the Isthmus," Vol. 36, No. 5532, p 2,
    18 December 1868. 21 March 2015.
"Special Correspondence," Vol. 2, No. 225, p 2,
    9 December 1851. 5 April 2014.
"Territorial Meeting in Honey Lake Valley." Vol. 14,
    No. 2048, p 1. 19 October 1857. 26 May 2014.

Online Newspaper Archives - Other

Daily Union, "Arrival of Immigrants by the Shasta
  Route," Vol. 3, No. 433, p 2, 26 August   1852.
  Sacramento. http://cdnc.ucr.edu. 19 April 2014.

Daily Union, "The Fire at Shasta," Vol. 4, No. 537, p 2,
  13 December 1852. Sacramento. http://cdnc.ucr.
  edu. 20 April 2014.

Huron Reflector, "California Items," p 2, May 8, 1849.
  Norwalk, Huron County, OH. http://home.
  ancestry.com. 3 May 2015.

Huron Reflector, "Interesting Letters From California,"
  p 1, August 13, 1850. Norwalk, Huron County,
  OH. http://home.ancestry.com/. 3 May 2015.

Marin Journal, "From the Mines," Vol. 1, No. 17, p 2,
  3 July 1861. San Rafael, Marin County, CA. http://
  cdnc.ucr.edu. 27 December 2014.

Marysville Daily Herald, "From the Plains," Vol. IV,
  No. 6, p 2, 13 August 1853. Marysville, CA.
  http://cdnc.ucr.edu. 6 June 2015.

Marysville Daily Herald, "Rains and Crops at Honey
  Lake," Vol. VII, No. 263, p 2, 15 June   1857.
  Marysville, CA. http://cdnc.ucr.edu. 25 May 2014.

Nevada Observer, "Nevada History: Without
  Government 1857," Online News Magazine,
  Nevada. Ch VII, p 42, 26 December 2005. http://
  www.nevadaobserver.com. 26 May 2014.

New York Tribune, The Library of Congress, Chronicling
  America. "General News," Vol. XXII, No. 6750.
  P 1, 21 November 1862. New York City. http://
  chroniclingamerica.loc.gov. 2 August 2, 2014.

SUSANVILLE

New York Times, "Marine Intelligence: Cleared. Arrived. By Telegraph. Foreign Ports," 22 November 1862, New York City. 03 August 2014. http://www.nytimes.com/1862/11/22/news/marine-intelligence-cleared-arrived-by-telegraph-foreign-ports.html.

Richland Shield and Banner, "California Intelligence," Vol. IX, No. 51, p 3, 29 May 1850.Mansfield, Richland County, OH. http://news.google.com/newspapers. 12 April 2014.

Sacramento Transcript, "The Tragedy at Shasta City," Vol. 3, No. 4, p 2, 3 April 1851.Sacramento. http://cdnc.ucr.edu. 3 May 2014.

Sacramento Transcript, "The Place they Pick up Lumps," Vol. 2, No. 60, p 2, 4 January 1851. Sacramento. http://cdnc.ucr.edu. 5 April 2014.

Wayne County Democrat, "The Wonders of American Energy," Vol. 6, No. 5, p 2, 18 April,1850. Wooster, OH. http://news.google.com/newspapers. 12 April 2014.

Weekly Alta California, "Election Returns," Vol. 3, No. 321, p 3, 20 November 1852. San Francisco. http://cdnc.ucr.edu. 9 April 2014.

Online Sources

American Mule Museum, *History of the Mule*, 2015, http://mulemuseum.org/History_of_the_Mule.html. 3 January 2015.

Baughman, Abraham J. *History of Ashland County, Ohio*, S. J. Clark Publishing Company. 1909, pp. 64-65. http://books.google.com. 6 September 2014.

Bristow, Kathi. *Those Daring Stage Drivers*. California State Parks, 2008. http://www.parks.ca.gov/?page_id=25451. 30 August 2014.

CAGenWeb Project. *Lassen County Biographies.*
Transcribed from *Illustrated History of Plumas,
Lassen & Sierra Counties, with California from
1513 to 1850* (Fariss and Smith, San Francisco,
1882) p 400, 2006. http://www.cagenweb.com/
lassen/bio2.htm. 26 October 2014.

California Bound. *Passenger Lists for California 1848
– 1873.* Sfgenealogy. http://www.sfgenealogy.
com/californiabound/cbindex.htm 25 Sept. 2013.
2 March 2014.

California Bound. *Passengers from the East. Orizaba
Passenger List December 1862.* SF Genealogy
2008. http://www.sfgenealogy.com/
californiabound/cb204.htm. 2 March 2014.

California Department of Parks and Recreation.
*Strawberry Valley House – Overland Pony
Express Route in California.* 2014. http://ohp.
parks.ca.gov/ListedResources/Detail/707.
30 August 2014.

Chandler, Katherine, "San Francisco at Statehood," *San
Francisco Chronicle.* 9 September 1900. http://www.
sfmuseum.org/hist5/oldsf.html. 24 August 2014.

Forest History Society. *History of Tahoe National
Forest: 1840-1940. The Era of Individual
Enterprise: Mining and Settlement on Tahoe
National Forest Lands, 1848-1859.* Chapter III,
6 August 2010. http://www.foresthistory.org/
ASPNET/Publications/region/5/tahoe/chap3.htm.
13 June 2015.

GlobalSecurity.org. *Nicaragua Railway and Canal 1849-
1871.* http://www.globalsecurity.org/military/
facility/panama-canal-nicaragua-1.htm. 2000-
2014. 17 April 2014.

SUSANVILLE

Guinn, James Miller. *History of the State of California and Biographical Record of the Sierras: An Historical Story of the State's Marvelous Growth from Its Earliest Settlement to the Present Time.* Chapman Publishing Company, 1906. Pp 322-323, 335, 1558, 1584, 1668, 1671. http://books.google.com/ 11 May 2014.

IAGenWeb Project. *Keokuk County Iowa. Jackson Township Biographical Directory*, 1997, http://iagenweb.org/keokuk/biographies/jackson_twp.html. 24 May 2014.

IAGenWeb. *Iowa in the Civil War. 7th Iowa Infantry History.* 2002-2003. http://iagenweb.org/civilwar/regiment/infantry/07th/7th-inf-hist.htm. 25 October 2014.

IAGenWeb. *Iowa Seventh Infantry.* Keokuk County Iowa, 1997-2015. http://iagenweb.org/keokuk/military/7th_infantry.htm. 16 February 2015.

Logan, Guy E. *Historical Sketch Seventh Regiment Iowa Volunteer Infantry.* Roster and Record of Iowa Troops In the Rebellion, Vol. 1. 8 February 2014. http://iagenweb.org/civilwar/books/logan/mil309.htm 16 February 2015.

Maritime Heritage Project, *Ships, Passengers, Captains Sailing into San Francisco from World Seaports during the 1800s.* http://www.maritimeheritage.org. 25 September 2013.

National Park Service. *Soldiers and Sailors Database,* 4 July 2014.http://www.nps.gov/civilwar/soldiers-and-sailors-database.htm. 13 July 2014.

National Park Service. *Battle Unit Details.* Union Iowa Volunteers. 7th Regiment Iowa Infantry, 4 July 2014. 19 July 2014. http://www.nps.gov/civilwar/search-battle-units- detail.htm?battleUnitCode=UIA0007RI.

National Park Service. *Battle Unit Details.* Union Ohio Volunteers. 23rd Regiment Ohio Infantry, 4 July 2014. 19 July 2014. http://www.nps.gov/civilwar/search-battle-units-detail.htm?battleUnitCode=UOH0023RI.

National Park Service. *National Register of Historic Places.* Ormsby-Rosser House. 26 March1979. *http://focus.nps.gov/pdfhost/docs/NRHP/Text/79003437.pdf.* 28 December 2015.

Nevada. *Laws of the Territory of Nevada Passed at the First Regular Session of the Legislative Assembly.* Pp. xviii, 264-265. Valentine & Company, 1862. http://books.google.com/.

Ohio Genealogy Express. *Ashland County Ohio,*2008. http://www.ohiogenealogyexpress.com/ashland/ashlandco_twps.htm. 5 Nov. 2013

Pacific Mail Steamship Company. *Central Pacific Railroad Photographic History Museum.* CPRR.org. 2013. http://cprr.org/Museum/Ephemera/Pacific_Mail_Steamship_Co.html. 25 September 2013.

Panama Railroad, *The Panama Railroad & the US Mail.* http://www.panamarailroad.org/mail.html. 17 August 2014.

Pastfinder, Quarterly Newsletter of the Ashland County Chapter of the Ohio Genealogical Society. http://ashlandohiogenealogy.org/pastfinder/pastfinderashlandcounty.html
——*Gold Rush Diary of G. W. King.* Vol. 5 Issue 2 p 22. May 1986. March 23, 2014.
——*Gold Rush Diary of G. W. King.* Vol. 24 Issue 3 pp. 1-3. August 2005. January 4, 2014.
——*Gold Rush Diary of G. W. King.* Vol. 24 Issue 4 pp. 38-40. November 2005. January 5, 2014.

SUSANVILLE

——*List of Letters*. Vol. 7 Issue 2 p 21. May 1988. March 30, 2014.

——*Queries*. Vol. Issue 4 p 47. August 1990. March 30, 2014.

——*The Visit*. Vol. 5 Issue 3 p 27. August 1986. February 16, 2014.

Perrin, William Henry, Battle, J.H. *History of Morrow County and Ohio*. *1880*. Baskin & Company, Morrow County, Ohio. Pp. 435, 476. http://books. google.com/. 26 April, 2015.

Peterson, Carol and Peter Uzelac, *Trips into History*. Historic Stories and Travel Ideas. 25 January 2013. http://tripsintohistory.com/2013/01/25/sacramento-history-the-steamboat/. 30 August 2014.

Pennsylvania Genealogy and Facts, *Allegheny County, Pennsylvania Facts, Records & Links*, 2014. http://www.genealogyinc.com/pennsylvania/ allegheny-county. 1 Apr. 2014.

Postal Gazette, *The Panama Route, 1848-1851*. Issue 5, No. 2. November 2006. http://www.thepostalgazette. com/issues/5/ThePanamaRoute.pdf. 19 April 2014.

Potts, Allen L. *History of Ashland County Ohio. Dr. J. E. Roop*. Heritage Pursuit. 23 August 2015. http://www.heritagepursuit.com/Ashland/ Ashland1876P350.htm. 29 August 2015.

Purdy, Tim, *Lahontan Images Presents, Exploring Northeastern California History, Lassen County Obituary Index*. Susanville, CA. 21 November 2014, http://www.citlink. net/~lahontan/archivelinks/lassenobitindex.htm. 26 April 2015.

Richards, T. Addison. *Appleton's Companion Handbook of Travel*. D. Appleton & Company, New York. 1866, P 256. https://books.google.com/. 7 December 2014.

Root, Frank and William Connelley, *The Overland Stage to California*, Ch 3, p 1, 1901 http://www. memoriallibrary.com/CA/OSTC/Chapter3.htm. 30 August 2014.

Ruiz, Bruce. *The Argonauts*, Personal Page Bruce C. Ruiz, Sr. (1942-2003). 15 February 2002. http://www.bruceruiz.net/PanamaHistory/ argonauts.htm. 13 April 2014.

Schrantz, Scott. *Carsonpedia. St. Charles Hotel.* 20 June 2012. http://carsonpedia.com/St._Charles_Hotel. 6 September 2014.

Ship's List, *Steamships on the Panama Route – both Atlantic and Pacific.* 5 February 2005.http://www. theshipslist.com/ships/descriptions/panamafleet. shtml. 4 July 2014.

Smith, Dottie. *Taking Care of History; The long-gone Oak Bottom House.* Dottie Smith's Blog. 21 January 2010. http://blogs.redding.com/dsmith/ archives/2010/01/the-long-gone-o.html. 13 April 2014.

Yester Year Once More. *News from the Gold Country: Josiah Roop Writes Home.* 8 April 2009. http:// yesteryearsnews.wordpress.com/2009/04/08/ news-from-the-gold-country-josiah-roop-writes-home/. 13 April 2014

Photographs

Guinn, James Miller. *History of the State of California and Biographical Record of the Sierras: An Historical Story of the State's Marvelous Growth from Its Earliest Settlement to the Present Time.* "A.T. Arnold and Susan E. Roop Arnold," Chapman Publishing Company, 1906, 322. http:// books.google.com/. 11 May 2014.

SUSANVILLE

Harper's Weekly "New Iron Steamship Champion, *of the Vanderbilt Line."* Digital image. Library of Congress., v. 3, No. 144, P. 625., 1 Oct. 1859. http://www.loc.gov/pictures/item/2008676715/. 3 August 2014.

Jenks, Daniel A., Artist, 1827-1869. *Mountain Camp, Sierra Nevada.* Digital image. Library of Congress. Original: August 13, 1859. http://www. loc.gov/item/2004661642/. 14 June 2015.

Lassen County Historical Society, Susanville, CA.
    Arnold Planing Mill
    Constantia
    Freighting on Main Street
    Isaac Roop
    John V. Roop, Dr.
    Lassen County Pioneer Society
    Main Street Susanville 1864
    Northside of Main Street Looking East
    Old Livery Stable. North side of Main Street, Looking East
    Roop House, Old Fort Roop
    Roop Residence
    Stage Coach, George B. Long, Stage Driver
    Steward House
    Susan Roop
    Susan Roop Arnold

Lawrence & Houseworth, publisher. *Pioneer Stage. Leaving Wells, Fargo & Co.'s. C Street, Virginia City.* Digital image. Library of Congress. 1866. http://www.loc.gov/pictures/item/2002722014. 13 September 2014.

Lawrence & Houseworth, publisher. *Strawberry Valley Station, Placerville Route, Yuba County, California.* Digital image. Library of Congress. 1866. http://www.loc.gov/pictures/item/2002719810/.13 September 2014.

Lawrence & Houseworth, publisher. *View of the Procession.* Digital image. *Library of Congress.* Zakreski and Hartman. 1850. http://www.loc.gov/ item/2002711451/.13 June 2015.PGA - Zakreski & Hartman--View of the procession

Miles, Zellamae Arnold. *Main Street Susanville Looking East.* Postcard donated to Lassen County Historical Society, Susanville, CA.

Prang, L. & Co. Thulstrup, Thure de, 1848-1930, artist. *Battle of Antietam.* Digital image. Library of Congress. Original: December 19, 1887. http://ndl. loc.gov/loc.pnp/pga/04031. 23 May 2015.

Public Records

Certificate of Marriage, Alexander Arnold and Susan Roop. Lassen County Recorder's Office, Court House, Susanville, CA. Julie Bustamante Clerk/ Recorder, Sarah Howe, Deputy Recorder. 20 January 2015.

Research

Pastfinder, The Quarterly Newsletter of the Ashland County Chapter of the Ohio Genealogical Society. *Gold Rush Diary of G. W. King.* Vol. 24, Issue 2, pp 19-20, May 2005. Research by Pam Blaha, Wayne County Historical Society. March 23, 2014.

Pastfinder, The Quarterly Newsletter of the Ashland County Chapter of the Ohio Genealogical Society. *Gold Rush Diary of G. W. King.* Vol. 24, Issue 3, pp 25-27. August 2005. Research by Pam Blaha, Wayne County Historical Society. March 23, 2014.

SUSANVILLE

Pastfinder, The Quarterly Newsletter of the Ashland
County Chapter of the Ohio Genealogical Society.
Gold Rush Diary of G. W. King. Vol. 24, Issue
4, pp 38-39. November 2005. Research by Pam
Blaha, Wayne County Historical Society.
March 23, 2014.

Pastfinder, The Quarterly Newsletter of the Ashland
County Chapter of the Ohio Genealogical Society.
Gold Rush Diary of G. W. King. Vol. 25, Issue 1
pp 2-4. February 2006. Research by Pam Blaha,
Wayne County Historical Society. March 23, 2014.

Past Lane, *John Gardner Family and Susan Roop*. Cheryl
Brown Abernathy CG, Research.10353 Sterling
Road, Fredericksburg, OH, 44627. 28 May, 2014.

Wayne County Genealogical Society. *The Dorland Party
Rowsburg, Ohio*. Pam Blaha, Research. PO Box
856, Wooster, OH 44691. September 20, 2013.

Unpublished Materials

Arnold, Greg, *Interview and Correspondence*. Susanville,
CA. September 20, 2013.

Kirov, George. *Roop, Isaac N.*, Lassen College Library,
Susanville, CA, circa 1980. 9 May 2014.

Lassen County Historical Society, *Genealogy of the
Isaac Newton Roop Family*. Prepared by Jack
Burk. Susanville, CA. August 28, 2012.

Lassen County Historical Society. *Isaac Roop*. Prepared
by Faye Messinger. Susanville, CA.July 11, 2015.

Lassen County Historical Society. *Isaac Roop, Shasta
City and Susanville California Correspondence*.
Susanville, CA. 6 June 2014.

Lassen County Historical Society. *Peace Meeting*.
Susanville, CA. 26 December 2015

Lassen County Historical Society. *Medford Roop Arnold.* Susanville, CA. 26 December 2015.

Miles, Zellamae Arnold. *Interview, Correspondence, Family Genealogy.* Susanville, CA. October 13, 2013.

Purdy, Tim, *Email correspondence.* Lassen County Historian, Susanville, CA. January 3, 4, 7, 22, 2014. June 28, 2014. July 24, 2014.

Roop, Isaac, *Roop House Register.* August 1854. Viewed on microfiche at Lassen County Public Library, Susanville, CA, 9 November 2013.

SUSANVILLE

Index

A

B

SUSANVILLE

H

Honey Lake Rangers 158, 163
Honey Lake Valley 5, 13, 42, 53-60, 69-71, 75-77, 79-82,
    90, 99, 111-112, 114, 116, 119, 122, 129, 142-144,
    146, 148-149, 151-152, 156-157, 168, 171, 203, 210
Honey Lake Wagon Road 147, 152-153
Humboldt 120, 142, 152, 155-157, 206
Humboldt Exchange 93
Humboldt Mining District 152
Humboldt Region 92
Humboldt River 25, 42-43, 56, 87, 144, 152-153
Humboldt Sink 71, 144
Humbug 120

I

Idaho 156-157, 163, 166, 168
Illinois River 169
Independence, Missouri 25, 41-42, 46
Invalid Corps 118-119, 127
Iowa 54, 59-62, 65-69, 73, 84-86, 90, 94, 106, 123, 126-
    128, 148, 154, 161-162, 179, 189, 195-196, 210-212

J

Jackson County, Iowa 126
Janesville 82, 112, 130

K

Kentucky 17, 94, 161
Keokuk County, Iowa 60, 65, 68-69, 84, 162, 179, 195-196

L

M

SUSANVILLE

S

SUSANVILLE